Welcome Home

The Best of Today's Creative Home Arts

CREATIVE
HOME
ARTS
—CLUB—

Creative Home Arts Library™

Welcome Home

The Best of Today's Creative Home Arts

Printed in 2004.

Creative Director

Tom Carpenter

Book Design & Production

Julie Cisler

Senior Book Development Coordinator

Jen Weaverling

Managing Editor

Heather Koshiol

Contributing Writers

Connie Bastyr
Katie Bratsch
Jan Eisner
Doreen Howard
Marcene Kruger
Janel Leatherman
Terry Monahan
Cheryl Natt
Kelly March O'Hara
Greg and Jan Page
Ellen Spector Platt
Koren Russell
Connie Steinberg
Kathleen Stoehr
Steve and Kathryn Vork Waryan
Beth Wheeler

Contributing Photographers

Custom Building Products
Alan and Linda Detrick
ESTO
Mike Hendrickson
High Country Gardens
Jackson & Perkins
Moonshadow
Munroe Studio, Inc.
Nichols Garden Nursery
Greg Page
Park Nursery
Park Seed Co.
Style Solutions
White Flower Farm

Special Thanks To:

Mike Billstein
Terry Casey
Janice Cauley

2 3 4 5 6 / 08 07 06 05 04

ISBN 1-58159-223-X

© 2004 Creative Home Arts Club

Creative Home Arts Club
12301 Whitewater Drive
Minnetonka, Minnesota 55343
www.creativehomeartsclub.com

Contents

Introduction

Vintage Checkerboard Table, page 70

　　　　Welcome Home

Snow Dolls, page 52

Arts for you. We at the Creative Home Arts Club wanted to share and celebrate your Club magazine's "best of the best." It wasn't easy to narrow down to the exclusive craft, decorating, transformation and how-to projects you'll find on the pages that follow. But somehow we did it. For you. And we hope you love the result.

We also hope you love the results you get

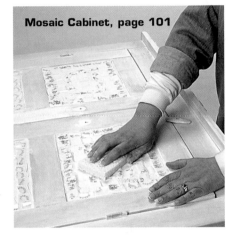

Mosaic Cabinet, page 101

when you explore these projects — maybe again, maybe for the first time because you never got a chance before. Now, in book form, they're yours forever.

I n looking back at a year's worth of your Club's award-winning magazine, *Today's Creative Home Arts,* it becomes quite clear that the projects, ideas, insights and instructions are worth saving. Beautiful pictures of the finished creations, instructive and clear photographs that guide you step by step to crafting and decorating success, hundreds of unique and beautiful ideas … it's all worthy of a book!

Those are the reasons behind the creation of *Welcome Home — The Best of Today's Creative Home*

So get ready to create some joy — when you make these projects with your own hands … and when you show off the final results to say *Welcome Home* to family, friends, guests and yourself.

CREATIVE
HOME
ARTS
—CLUB—

Decorative Throw Pillows, page 108

Chapter one
Crafts

Part of crafting's allure is the variety of projects you can complete with your own two hands, a few basic materials, and a little time.

Centerpiece for Winter

This rustic centerpiece catches and reflects light beautifully, and is elegant enough to leave out all season.

Welcome Home

There is something about the flicker of candlelight that creates a particularly homey atmosphere on cold winter nights.

Maybe it has to do with an age-old instinct to huddle around dancing flames, drawing closer both to the warmth and to others as we share stories and food. Whatever the reason, one of the constants of a welcoming table is candles, used to enhance the atmosphere and, literally, to shed a warm light on all who gather to join in a meal.

This easy centerpiece takes advantage of the warm light of candles, but uses the soft glint of copper to bounce the light from the flames back and forth, creating a lovely effect.

Best of all, this centerpiece is attractive enough to use over and over, spending time between meals sitting on a mantel or in the center of the table. It will cost less than $25 to make, and will provide hours of elegance in return.

To Make This Centerpiece For Winter You Will Need:

◆ An old copper chafing or fondue pan with stand
◆ Grapevine wreath*
◆ Several packages of copper wire in varying weights*
◆ Copper screen (for wrapping candles)
◆ Thin sheets of copper craft material*
◆ Gold and silver craft paint*
◆ Rubber stamp (we used one with a grape cluster)*
◆ Three 3-inch candles of varying heights
◆ Small decorative push pins
◆ Several clusters of plastic grapes with leaves*
◆ Irridescent marbles*
◆ Scissors or tin snips
◆ Paintbrush
◆ Ballpoint pen
◆ Heavy gloves

*These can be found at any craft or hobby store. Copper wire can be purchased in the electrical section of any hardware store.

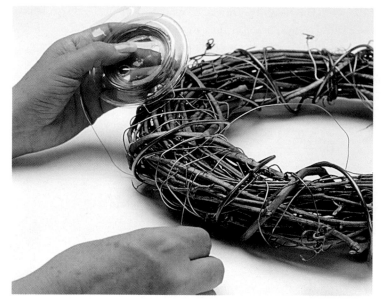

1 Remove a section of copper wire from packaging. Secure the wire around the wreath, twisting ends in on underside and tying in a knot. Gently wind the wire around the wreath in an uneven pattern. We used several packages of wire in different weights (widths) for this wreath, including some 10-gauge copper wire usually used for electrical work. This copper wire will catch and reflect light from the centerpiece, giving the wreath a unique appearance.

2 After you have finished winding the wire around the wreath, use a paintbrush dipped alternately in gold and silver craft paint to lightly feather additional color on the wreath. Do not paint the entire wreath; you want some of the natural grapevine material to show through. Set wreath aside to dry.

3 Put on a pair of heavy gloves for this part, because the copper screen has a sharp edge. Unroll a section of screen and lay one candle on it. Mark the upper and lower edge of the candle on the screen with a ballpoint pen. Remove candle, and use either a sharp scissors or a pair of tin snips to cut out a section of screen wide enough to roll around the candle, and tall enough to reach about an inch above and below each pen mark. Gently crease back a 1-inch portion at the top and bottom of the screen, folding to pen marks, to form a seam. (This will fold in the sharp edges.) Use your gold or silver craft paint to smooth some additional color on the screen, if desired. Repeat for each candle.

4 (optional) To decorate your candles further, you can add embossed copper cutouts.

To add the cutouts, snip out a small section of the thin copper material in a shape slightly larger than your rubber stamp. We selected a stamp with a grape cluster pattern. Ink the stamp and press it firmly against a piece of paper, cut slightly smaller than the copper. Tape paper to back (non-shiny) side of the copper. Use a ballpoint pen to trace over the stamp outline, pressing firmly. This creates an embossed pattern of the stamp on the front of the copper. Use a scissors to cut around the embossed area. (Be careful; the edges of the copper may be sharp.) Repeat for all candles, if desired.

6 (optional) Use additional gold or silver craft paint on the clusters of plastic grapes and leaves.

5 Lay candles on premeasured and pre-folded sections of screen. Roll screen around candles, securing in place with decorative push pins. Use additional push pins to secure optional copper cutouts to the side of each candle.

SPECIAL TIP

A centerpiece for a table should be short enough to see over and around easily. In general, the centerpiece should stand no higher than the distance from your elbow to your fingertips as your elbow rests on the tabletop.

NOTE

As with all candles, never leave this centerpiece burning unattended. As candles burn down, copper screen may become hot. If the candle burns below the screen edge, blow out the candles and let cool. Unpin the screen, snip off excess from the top, trim candle, and refold the screen again to provide a non-sharp edge.

7 Place grapevine wreath on table. Set legs of copper chafing dish inside wreath. Set candles inside copper chafing dish, and use irridescent marbles to fill in around the candles. Make sure candles sit securely inside dish so that they will not tip. Use plastic grapes and leaves to fill area around the base of the chafing dish legs. Tuck a few marbles into the wreath, and scatter additional marbles around the base of the wreath to catch and reflect light.

Rustic Wind Chime

This clever grapevine wind chime will sway and move with the slightest breeze.

Decorating for winter is one of the better parts of the season. This fun, attractive, and country-inspired wind chime will both welcome guests at your front door and brighten your entryway.

This clever wind chime is designed to move and sway with the slightest breeze. And because the grapevine base and attached foam fruits are suspended using thin wire and clear fishing line, the entire piece gives the illusion of a tree with the decorations suspended in midair.

We used a wrought-iron candle stand to display our chime, but you can adapt this technique for a similar chime without it. Instead, make a simple wire loop at the top of the piece and hang the chime from a secure ceiling hook. Either way, this fun piece will delight you and your visitors. In a semi-sheltered position, it will also last beautifully until spring. The cost for this piece without the candle stand was less than $40 for materials.

To Create a Rustic Wind Chime You Will Need:

◆ Several plain grapevine wreaths, in graduated sizes*
◆ Paintbrush
◆ Small amount of white craft paint
◆ Thin, strong florist's wire**
◆ Ruler
◆ Blue painter's tape
◆ Safety glasses
◆ Metal candle stand***
◆ Drill with ⅜-inch metal bit**
◆ A variety of small foam fruits**
◆ Transparent fishing line
◆ A thin nail or rigid piece of wire (for piercing fruit)
◆ Hot-glue gun
◆ Small bells
◆ Raffia
◆ Silk flowers/berries

*Note: For our chime, we selected six different-sized grapevine wreaths, graduated in size from smallest (about 4 inches in diameter) to largest (about 30 inches in diameter). The size and number of wreaths you use is up to you. The important thing is that each wreath you select is slightly smaller than the wreath that will hang below it. We experimented with a variety of wreaths at our local craft store by "stacking them" on top of each other to find a pleasing arrangement.

** These items are available at craft or floral stores.

***We made a rather large, six-wreath wind chime for use on a porch. We created it around a metal candle stand designed for a pillar candle. We used our candle stand by drilling three holes through the outer edge of the pillar base with a metal bit to accommodate the hanging wires from the wreath. You can make a smaller wind chime and omit these steps by simply hanging your grapevine wind chime from a secure ceiling hook with wire. (This option works best for a smaller, lighter wind chime with up to four wreaths.) See alternate directions in Step 6. To keep our chime from tipping over in a strong breeze, we placed the base of the stand firmly in a bucket of sand disguised with burlap.

SPECIAL TIP

Before you start

Once you're ready to begin, lay your wreaths on top of each other on a flat surface in order of size. Make sure each wreath sits naturally on the wreath below it.

Using a paintbrush, put a tiny dab of white craft paint at one point in the middle of the vines on the top of the largest wreath. (See image in Step 1.) Make a dot on the wreath above that to align with the dot on the wreath below it. Continue until all of the wreaths have a "line" of dots in a similar location. (This will simply help you to keep the wreaths centered and hanging equally when you begin to attach the wire.)

Each wreath will be attached with wire in three spots to the wreath above and below it. Imagine a triangle with the dots of white paint at one corner of the figure, and then add two more dots of paint on the wreaths at the other corners. This way, each wreath will have wire attached in roughly the same spot.

1 Lay your largest wreath on a flat surface. We wanted each of our wreaths to hang about 7½ inches apart once we were finished. Your measurements may vary, depending on how you plan to display your piece, and how many wreaths you will attach.

We clipped three pieces of florist's wire about 30 inches long, and then twisted them together into double strands 15 inches long (doubling the wire makes it stronger). We then attached each of these strands to our largest wreath over each dot of paint, wrapping the wire around two or three strong pieces of grapevine and then tying.

This gave us three lengths of wire, each at one corner of an imaginary triangle on our wreath.

2 Since we wanted our wreaths to hang 7½ inches apart, we marked that point on our wire with a piece of painter's tape. We then tied the free end of the wire from our first wreath securely to the UNDERSIDE of the next largest wreath. (The dots of paint will serve as a visual aid to help you find the correct spot for attaching the wire.) We made each of our knots underneath the wreath as close as we could to the painter's tape.

Once the first two wreaths are firmly secured together with all three pieces of wire, hold them up and check to make sure that the first wreath hangs naturally from the wreath above it. Once you are satisfied, clip off any excess wire.

3 Continue attaching the wreaths as described above, until you have all of your wreaths securely tied together. Periodically check your progress by holding up the entire piece to make sure that the wreaths hang naturally.

When you reach what will be your top wreath, do not clip any excess wire for the moment.

4 (Optional) We wanted to display our wind chime on the floor by using a metal pillar candle stand as a support for our wreaths. These stands are available for under $50 at decorative accessory stores or large discount stores. However, you can skip this step and proceed to Step 6 if you prefer to make a smaller hanging wind chime.

Put on safety glasses. Using a drill and a ⅜-inch metal drill bit, make three holes in the thin metal candle support of the stand at each corner of an imaginary triangle, drilling each hole about ¾ inch from the outside edge.

5 If your wreath display is a large one, have a friend help with this step.

Set the candle support upright and have your friend hold it securely. Lift your wreath display and using the excess wire on the top wreath, thread this through the holes in the candle display and tie securely.

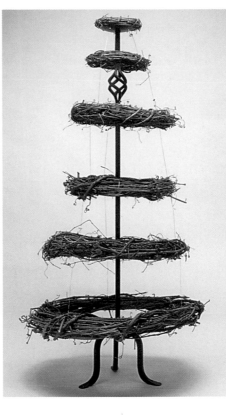

6 If you are using the candle stand to support your wreath tree, the piece should look like this at this point.

If you aren't using the candle stand to support your wreath, create a "hanger" at the top of the piece by tying the remaining wire from your top wreath together.

(Note: You must provide extra support for the base of this stand before displaying it to keep the piece from tipping over in a strong wind. To do this, place the base of the stand in a large, deep container, fill the container with sand, and hide the support by wrapping the base with burlap and tying with raffia.)

7 Select an arrangement of small, colorful, foam fruit. These fruits will be suspended below each wreath on a few inches of clear fishing line, giving the impression that they are hanging in air.

There are two ways to proceed with this step. We found that piercing a hole through the foam fruit with a thin nail or piece of rigid wire let us thread the end of our fishing line through the hole. We then secured the line with a dab of hot glue both on the top and bottom of the fruit for the greatest security. You can simply hot-glue your fishing line to the top of each piece of fruit and skip piercing it, but you may find that some pieces will blow off the wind chime in a heavy breeze. The choice is yours.

8 Once you have attached your fruits to lengths of fishing line, tie them in a random assortment around the grapevine wreaths. You will notice that the fruits bob and move whenever wind hits the wreaths.

9 To finish your wind chime, create small bows from raffia and hot-glue them in place around the piece. (These bows can be used to disguise the points where you have attached your wire.) Use silk berries to drape around the wreath to create a softer appearance. Use raffia to secure small bells below each wreath, where the breeze will make them ring. Add small silk birds or other decorations if you wish.

Pressed-Flower Table

Dried pansies accent an elegant occasional table.

One of the easiest and most inexpensive ways to create a unique personal decor is to use items you already have in an unusual, attractive way.

This pressed-pansy table is a perfect example of that philosophy. It adds a touch of color to any room, is the perfect springtime accent piece, and you can also assemble it from

items you probably already have in your house—or, for that matter, out in your garden.

To create this pressed-pansy table, you will need an inexpensive three-legged round table with a glass onlay. You can purchase these tables, along with a piece of tempered glass already cut to size, for less than $20 at almost any discount store. They are made of pressed wood, and are designed to be covered by a circular tablecloth, also available at those same stores. These tables are small and versatile, and work beautifully tucked next to a favorite reading chair.

Better yet, the glass tabletop makes these tables practical. The glass resists marks from water glasses or other scuffing, keeping the tablecloth beneath clean. But for our purposes, the glass top also offers another benefit: You can use this glass cover as a frame for a wide variety of pressed flowers or other natural materials. Because it takes only minutes to remove the top and change the arrangement beneath, you can also bring the outdoors inside throughout the spring, summer, and fall, letting you change the look of the piece at will.

Here we show how to use this table and topper to showcase pressed pansies, a perfect springtime flower, but that's just the start. You can use this technique on a variety of items. Consider pressing rose petals and arranging those bits of color in a fanciful garland around the edge of the table. Or use a combination of materials such as dried fern fronds and flat-petaled flowers such as tiny marigolds. Arrange the flowers along the stems of the fronds for a plant not found in nature! Or consider a fall arrangement with colorful dried red and yellow leaves twining around the edge of the table.

There are many ways to press flowers, but none are easier—or more low-tech—than to carefully dry them in an old telephone book. You will find that the flowers lose their color over time, but that's fine, because this display is meant to change with the seasons, and with your choices. If the table is not in direct sunlight, the colors of the blossoms will last longer.

(And a final tip: We used dried eucalyptus to form the green "leaves" on our pansies because they are versatile and hold their color well. You can use these pieces over again with other flowers.)

To Make a Pressed-Flower Table You Will Need:

◆ Three-legged accent table (available at any home or discount store)
◆ Glass table-topper
◆ Dried flowers and other natural materials*
◆ Old telephone book
◆ Scissors
◆ Several pieces of dried eucalyptus

* Consider using petals from a wide variety of flowers and then creating your own "blooms" by drying the petals, arranging them on the tablecloth, and adding "leaves" made from eucalyptus. You can also create a unique look for your table using dried flowers arranged on unusual greenery—such as tiny marigolds along the stem of dried fern fronds, or rose petals atop spiky iris greens. Use your imagination.

1 Press any variety of flat-petaled flowers in a phone book until dry. Remove flowers carefully, and cut eucalyptus leaves off to create "leaves" for your dried flowers.

2 Arrange flowers in a pattern or randomly on the tablecloth over the table. Select eucalyptus leaves in sizes that look natural alongside dried pansies.

3 Place eucalyptus both beneath and between petals. Leave some flowers plain; give others several "leaves."

4 Once you're happy with your arrangement, place the glass top over the flowers. Change the flowers often to match the seasons.

Ribbon & Rose Wreath

This easy-to-make wreath will chase away winter blues and, when dried, will last all season.

Roses in winter are an ideal treat to help lift spirits or make any occasion extra-special. You can make this wreath in honor of Valentine's Day, or just to brighten your home for any occasion.

Follow the instructions to create a wreath exactly like this one, but don't feel that you have to stop there: There are lots of options to help you personalize this type of wreath to commemorate a special event, or just to meet your own taste preferences.

For instance, use pastel pink roses and a bright pink bow to celebrate the winter birthday of a special little girl. White roses and a white satin bow add elegance to a winter wedding or shower. When you add baby's breath flowers to this wreath, it looks like a sudden snow shower. If you're not a fan of baby's breath, omit it. Add some small pinecones instead, or add whatever winter greens you have available. Boxwood and arborvitae are both lovely and long-lasting, and you may be able to

find some right out your front door. Substitute preserved eucalyptus for fresh if your florist offers a good price on the former. For a less-expensive wreath, use fewer roses in a more regular pattern, or for a more extravagant wreath, add dozens. The final look depends on what you like.

Once you've finished your wreath, you can hang it on an outside door if temperatures stay above freezing. Otherwise hang the wreath in a cool spot—an inside door or window works well. (Don't hang your fresh wreath over a fireplace or heat register because the warmth will hasten the demise of the fresh roses.)

If your roses are very fresh when you buy them, recut the stems under water, place them in a vase of water, and give them a long drink—at least 12 hours or so—before making the wreath (see Step 2). That way, your wreath will look fresh for five to seven days or more.

Best of all, the materials in this wreath will gradually dry while hanging and continue to look well, if not as sprightly as when first made. Roses will sometimes dry in place without the need to reposition them, but if your roses begin to slide loose as they dry, simply replace them and secure more tightly.

As a final note, you might try the rose variety Mercedes because it dries to a true and beautiful red.

To Make a Ribbon & Rose Wreath You Will Need:

- Fresh cut pine boughs
- Fresh eucalyptus
- 15 or more bright red roses
- Floral food
- Baby's breath (optional)
- One 14-inch vine wreath base
- Small florist water tubes with caps, one for each rose (reusable, and available from your local florist)
- Florist reel wire
- Scissors or clippers
- Ribbon bow and extra 24 inches of ribbon
- Stapler

HOW TO BUY FRESH ROSES

Did you know that much like supermarket lettuce or herbs, roses also have a limited shelf life? You will gain three to four days more enjoyment from your roses if you buy them from the florist the day they arrive. (It's even better if your florist bought the roses from the wholesaler the day they came in from the grower.) Call in advance and ask when the next delivery of roses comes in.

When you buy roses from a street vendor, grocery, or florist, remove the flowers from the water and look at the bottom of the stems. If they're dark and discolored or, heaven forbid, slimy, you know that they've been hanging around too long. If there is any sign of mold on the leaves, don't buy the flowers. You wouldn't buy peaches with soft brown spots or green beans that are turning brown, so exercise the same selectivity with flowers and you won't be disappointed.

1 Strip leaves off roses. Fill a sink with lukewarm water and immerse the stems. Recut each stem on a slant underwater with a sharp clippers or scissors. (By doing this, you prevent "air bubbles" from getting stuck in the flower stem. Air bubbles prevent roses from taking up water, and result in "droopy-necked" flowers.)

2 Once stems are recut, stand flowers in a bucket of water. For best results, add cut flower food to the water according to package directions.

3 Loop ribbon around the vine wreath base and staple the ends of the ribbon together. The wreath will hang from this loop when finished. Cut the greens into pieces about 8 inches long, discarding woody stems. Remove caps from the florist tubes, fill with water, and recap. Cut the roses to fit and insert each stem through the hole in the cap of a tube.

4 Tie the end of the reel wire onto the vine wreath base near the ribbon loop. The general procedure for making this wreath is to wrap a handful of greens onto the base, wrap them with wire while pulling the wire tightly, and then lay another handful over the stems of the handful before. Add roses in the same way, wrapping the tubes onto the base with the reel wire. Cover the tubes with additional greenery or baby's breath.

5 I made two versions of the wreath, the first with 15 roses in clusters of threes. The second version has 21 roses wrapped more or less at random. (It's okay if a little of the vine wreath base peeks out from among the greens; it only adds to the naturalness of the wreath.)

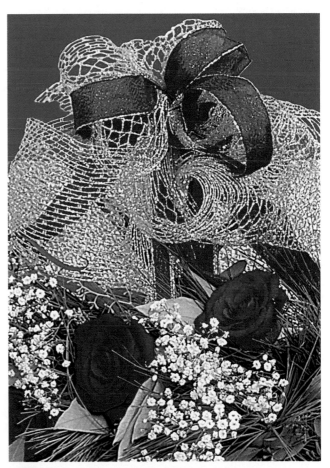

6 When you come full circle around the wreath, tie off the end of the wire at the back of the wreath. Hang on a hook or nail from the ribbon loop. Use the bow to cover the nail. If you use the optional baby's breath, tuck it in among the greens after the wreath is hanging in place.

Child's Bath Wrap

These easy-to-make bath wraps are ideal gifts for any youngsters on your list.

Stepping out of a warm bath and snuggling into a thick, fluffy robe is a wonderful way to end an evening.

Adults have long taken advantage of this special pleasure, but now, with a couple of hours' time and less than $20 in materials, you can share this experience with your favorite young person.

This easy-to-make bath wrap makes a perfect gift, too, especially if you combine it with a few favorite bath accessories and tuck in a few rubber duckies to keep your favorite little one company.

Best of all, you can pick colors and trims that match the tastes of the recipient. Have a little boy who sees himself as the captain of his own fleet? Pick a bright blue towel, trim it with gold braid, and you have an instant admiral. Know a little girl who's more sugar than spice? Use a soft pink color scheme, add a little lace trim and some heart-shaped appliques, and you'll create a treasured gift for a picture-perfect doll.

To Make a Child's Bath Wrap You Will Need:

◆ Fluffy bath towel and matching washcloth
◆ Thread
◆ Scissors
◆ Pins
◆ Decorative trim (1½ to 2 yards)
◆ Decorative appliques

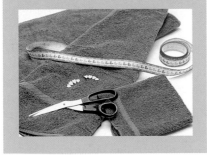

SPECIAL TIP

Egyptian cotton towels make the softest and fluffiest bathrobes. Laundering the towel, washcloth, and any embellishing trim before sewing will remove sizing and allow for shrinkage. (You may want to wash the trim by hand to avoid any color bleeding that may occur in the laundering process.) Avoid using fabric softener as it reduces the towel's absorbency.

1 Launder towel and washcloth and remove manufacturer's tags. Use a sharp scissors to cut tag close to towel.

2 For the hood: Place right sides of washcloth together (finished edge of hem to the inside). Fold back edge of washcloth to about ½ inch beyond woven band, making a cuff at the edge of the hood. Pin and sew in place.

3 With right sides of washcloth together, fold hood in half; pin and sew at opposite end of hemmed edge. Turn right side out.

4 To attach hood to the bath towel, locate and mark the center of the longest edge of the bath towel. With right sides together, match the center seam of the hood to the center of the bath towel. Pin each edge of hood to towel and sew in place. Turn robe right side out.

SPECIAL TIP

These robes are wonderful gifts for kids age five and younger. Fill a basket with tub toys and bubble bath, and tuck a teddy bear into the mix for a perfect gift.

5 To embellish the robe: Pin decorative trim in place on long edge of towel, following over the hood and down the other side of the towel. Sew both edges of trim. Use a longer stitch length to help eliminate any puckering of the trim.

6 Pin appliques at desired locations. Iron-on appliques should also be sewn in place to ensure stability through frequent laundering.

Two Decorator Clocks

Oversized, "decorator clocks" cost a fortune when purchased at a store. We made two versions for less than $40 each.

If you've glanced through any high-end home furnishing catalog recently, you've probably seen an abundance of oversized, "decorator-style" clocks, designed for both beauty and function. You may have also gasped at the price these clocks command—some versions sell for $300 and up!

We loved the look of these clever clocks, but were dismayed by the price. We decided to re-create the look and feel of these clocks ourselves, using simple materials in unique ways. We created two versions of these oversized clocks—the first, a Tuscan-inspired "wine clock" with a matching decorative shelf; the second, a "music" clock embellished with old sheet music.

Each of these clocks cost less than $40 to make, including the clockworks themselves, which we purchased from an Internet source specializing in everything for the home clock-making enthusiast. (See "A Word About Clocks" on page 25.) The projects can be completed in less than four hours, aside from drying time.

If you'd like to see time fly in a fashionable way this winter, we encourage you to visit your local home improvement store and get started right now!

A WORD ABOUT CLOCKS

Making personalized clocks is surprisingly easy once you have the mechanical portion of the clock itself. The mechanics of a clock include the motor, the hands, and a battery pack that powers the clock. These clockwork packages are readily available for a few dollars from a number of suppliers, and can be found at any craft or hobby store.

However, in some cases, you may find that the prepackaged sizes and dimensions of the clockworks available to you do not correspond to the size clock you would like to make. (Smaller clockworks seemed to be the rule when we visited our local stores.)

Since we wanted to make several oversized, decorator-version clocks, we turned to an Internet supplier called Klockit, www.klockit.com, which offers an abundance of clock parts at very reasonable prices. We were able to mix and match different hand sizes, numbers, and other items to create the look we wanted for each of our clocks. We were also able to purchase all of the mechanical parts for the clocks shown on these pages for less than $15 each. In addition, we used a dial template that we purchased from Klockit to help us position the numbers on our clock correctly.

(Before ordering materials, know the dimensions of the clock you want to make. For instance, for our 24-inch diameter Tuscan Wine Clock, we used 17 ½-inch hands, and a ⅝-inch, high torque quartz movement to power them. Complete instructions for selecting the proper-sized movement are available at Klockit's Web site, or you can call their toll-free number for help in finding the proper size mechanicals for your particular clock.)

You can request a catalog from Klockit by calling (800) 556-2548, or by writing Klockit, P.O. Box 636, Lake Geneva, WI, 53147-0636.

To Make a Tuscan Wine Clock You Will Need:

- Plastic drop cloth
- Scrap wood pieces
- 24-inch round particle-board circle*
- Spatula or putty knife
- Lightweight joint compound (We recommend purchasing the 90-minute, easy-sand variety.)
- Aluminum foil
- 100-grit sanding block
- Dry paintbrush or tack cloth
- Cloth measuring tape
- Nail
- Pencil
- Primer and acrylic paint
- Paintbrush
- Drill and ⁵⁄₁₆-inch drill bit

- Artist acrylic paints
- Clear mixing glaze
- Plastic plates
- Cotton rags
- Artist brushes (angle and round tip brushes)
- Black permanent marker
- Dial template **
- Ruler or yardstick
- 2-inch plastic number stencil***
- Grape motif stamps***
- Antiquing glaze (optional)
- Two heavy-duty picture hangers
- Clockworks and appropriate-sized hands (See "A Word About Clocks" above.)

Optional:
- Hanging Shelf Top
- One 24-inch pre-made shelf***
- Wood filler and spatula
- Grape motif ornamental wood appliques****
- Two pieces of 6-inch chain
- Four large, heavy-duty cup hooks
- Drill and ³⁄₃₂-inch bit
- One heavy-duty picture hanger

* These are available precut at home improvement stores.

** These help you place numbers correctly on the face of a clock, and are available where clock supplies are sold.

***These items are available at craft or hobby stores.

****These items are available at home improvement, craft, or hobby stores.

1 Spread a plastic drop cloth over your work surface. (This project is best done in an area where you can leave the clock undisturbed for several hours while the materials dry.)

Place a couple of thin pieces of scrap wood onto the drop cloth, and then set your particleboard circle on the wood. (This keeps the board slightly elevated from your work surface, giving you easy access to the edges of the circle.)

Using a spatula or putty knife, begin by spreading a thin layer of joint compound about ⅛ inch thick over the entire surface and sides of your particleboard. The compound needs to be reasonably smooth and uniform, but it does not need to be perfect.

Next, while the joint compound is still wet, loosely crumple a piece of aluminum foil and randomly "pounce" it over the entire surface. This will create a lightly textured surface.

2 Next, run the spatula or putty knife across the textured compound in a random pattern, slightly smoothing the surface. Continue working the surface, until you have achieved a texture you like. Let dry undisturbed according to manufacturer's directions.

Once the joint compound has dried completely, lightly sand the entire surface. Brush away any loose dust with a dry paintbrush or tack cloth. Paint the entire surface and edges of the board with primer, and let dry completely. (We used an antique-white tinted primer on our clock.)

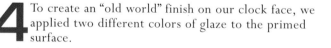

3 Locate the exact center of your circle. Drill a hole in the center of your board using an appropriately sized drill bit to accommodate the clock's quartz movement. We used a ⁵⁄₁₆-inch bit for our particular clock movement. Tip: Drill through your board from front to back to protect the prepared joint compound surface.

4 To create an "old world" finish on our clock face, we applied two different colors of glaze to the primed surface.

Our first coat of glaze used raw sienna acrylic pigment mixed in a ratio of 1 tablespoon of pigment color, 2 tablespoons of clear mixing glaze, and 4 tablespoons of water. Using a wide paintbrush, apply the glaze to the previously painted surface and edges, keeping your brush strokes random. While the glaze is still wet, lightly blot the surface of the clock face with a slightly damp cotton rag. For a more textured appearance, keep the marks left by the rag uneven by working in all directions. Let glaze dry completely.

Once our first layer of glaze was dry, we applied a second layer of olive green glaze. We mixed 1 tablespoon of olive green pigment/color, 2 tablespoons of clear mixing glaze and 4 tablespoons of water to create the glaze. Again, using a wide paintbrush, apply the glaze to the previously painted surface and edges, keeping your brush strokes random. You will now have a slightly mottled surface on your clock face. Before the second coat of glaze dries completely, move on to Step 5.

5 While the second coat of glaze is still wet, again lightly blot the surface of the clock face with a slightly damp cotton rag. For a more textured appearance, keep the marks left by the rag uneven by working in all directions.

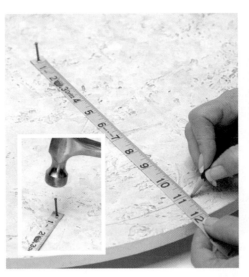

6 To create a perfect circle on your clock face, place a piece of scrap wood under the center of your particleboard. Place a nail through the end of a cloth measuring tape and tap the nail into the wood below. This will keep the measuring tape in place as you draw a circle.

Draw an inside circle 1¼ inches from the outside edge of your particleboard circle. (Rest a sharp pencil on the surface and pull the cloth measuring tape toward you, stopping at different intervals to turn the surface as you draw your line.)

7 Paint the outside circle and edges with two coats of acrylic artist paint, letting paint dry between coats. We used an olive green paint, and applied it using an angled artist's brush.

8 Once the paint is dry, draw a line around the inside edge of the previously painted circle, using a black permanent marker. Tip: Don't be concerned if the marker lines are slightly uneven. Due to the textured surface, the lines look more natural if they are slightly irregular.

9 Tape your clock face dial template in place in the center of clock using painter's tape. (See "A Word About Clocks" on Page 25.)

Extend the markings on the dial plate to the outside edges of the clock face using a yardstick or long ruler.

Using a sharp pencil, transfer the hour and minute placement to the clock face along the inside of the painted edge.

SPECIAL TIP

For accurate numeral placement, transfer the hour and minute placements by working from one side of the clock face to the other before moving the ruler to the next minute mark. For example: Make a mark at 12 and 6 o'clock, and then move your ruler slightly to transfer minute marks, and so on. It also helps to mark the hour placements using a piece of painter's tape. Finish by accentuating the minute markings using the tip of a black permanent marker.

10 Place your 2-inch number stencil on the clock face at the appropriate hour markings. Trace the correct number for hour marking using a sharp pencil. Use the minute markings as a guide to ensure that numbers are straight. Remove stencil, and check to ensure that the numbers are straight. Tip: A soft pencil eraser can be used to erase markings should you make any mistakes.

11 Paint the numbers on the clock face with black acrylic artist's paint. Let dry. Repeat with a second coat if necessary and let dry again.

Trace an additional inside circle, ½ inch from the bottom edge of the numbers, following instructions in Step 6. Cover this line with one or two coats of the same color paint you used on your outside circle. Tip: We found that round-tipped artist brushes produced the best results when painting delicate freehand work. Put a small amount of paint on the tip of a round tip brush and paint over pencil markings. Work slowly, using light brush strokes. Your line will be slightly uneven due to the textured surface.

12 Apply a decorative motif to the center of the clock face using decorator blocks, stencils or by painting in accents freehand. Here we used grape decorator sponge blocks and then added a wine bottle to the clock face freehand. Let dry. (You can use a round-tipped or fine pencil brush to apply additional detailing and highlights to your image. Let dry completely.)

13 To create a distressed, Old World-type finish, we randomly sanded the entire painted surface and edges using a 100-grit sanding block. This will remove and soften the paint in areas where you sand. You may wish to heavily or lightly distress the piece. The choice is yours. Remove any dust particles using a clean soft brush or tack cloth.

15 Once you're happy with your clock's appearance, protect the surface by applying two coats of acrylic sealer, letting the first coat dry before applying the second.

Assemble the mechanics of the clock following manufacturer's directions. Attach two heavy-duty picture hangers to the back of the clock, following manufacturer's instructions.

14 (Optional) You can further age your clock with an optional coat of antiquing glaze at this point. To do this, pour a small amount of antiquing glaze onto a plastic plate. Dip up a small amount of glaze with a slightly damp cotton rag and then rub the glaze onto the clock face. Work in small areas with a small amount of glaze at a time. Keep a clean damp cotton rag handy to remove any glaze that may have been applied too heavily.

SPECIAL TIP

This Tuscan Wine Clock will be heavy when finished. It's important to hang this clock as you would a heavy picture, using heavy-duty picture hangers on the back of the clock, and attaching it to the wall securely, using anchor bolts if necessary.

ADD A DECORATIVE SHELF TO YOUR WINE CLOCK

This is an optional project. We wanted to embellish our Tuscan Wine Clock by placing a decorative shelf above it, and tying the two items together visually using a grape motif. We also wanted to create the illusion that the clock face was "hanging" from the shelf on two pieces of chain.

To do this, we purchased a pre-made wooden shelf with three coat pegs on it at our local craft store. We unscrewed the wooden pegs from the shelf and filled the holes with wood filler. We then sanded, painted, and distressed the shelf following the same steps we used to paint the clock face.

We purchased two grape-shaped wooden appliques, painted them, and attached them to the center of our shelf using wood glue. We then added two large cup hooks about 8 inches apart at the bottom of our shelf. We placed similar cup hooks into the outside edge of the top of our clock face. We then visually connected our two elements by hooking a piece of plastic chain from the cup hook on the shelf to the cup hook on the clock.

NOTE: This chain is decorative only. The cup hooks cannot be used to suspend the clock face from the shelf because of the weight of the clock face. The shelf must be installed on the wall above the clock with its own heavy-duty picture hangers.

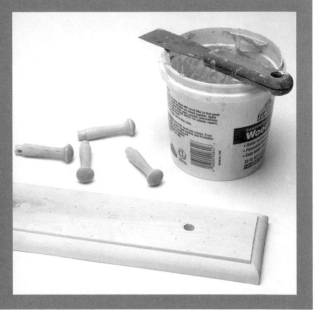

To Make an Old-Fashioned Music Clock You Will Need:

- ◆ Old music sheets
- ◆ Safety lighter*
- ◆ Heavy, heatproof gloves*
- ◆ 19-inch particleboard circle**
- ◆ Wallpaper paste or decoupage adhesive
- ◆ Medium-grit and fine-grit sandpaper
- ◆ Black acrylic artist paint/spray paint
- ◆ Paintbrush/sponge applicator
- ◆ Clock movement, hands, self-adhesive numbers***
- ◆ Copper finishing wax****
- ◆ Measuring tape or ruler
- ◆ Drill and appropriate drill bit
- ◆ Antiquing glaze (optional)
- ◆ Acrylic sealer

*See Special Note in Step 1.

**We used the top from an old, three-legged decorative table as the face for this clock. Simply unscrew the legs of the table and remove the connecting brackets.

***See "A Word About Clocks" on Page 25.

**** This is available at craft or art material stores.

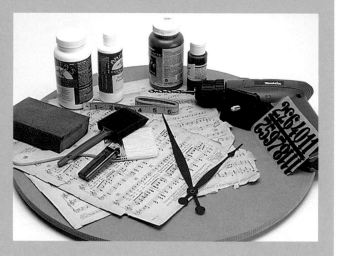

A WORD ABOUT MATERIALS

If you haven't paid a visit to your local hardware or home improvement store recently, now is the time. These stores offer an abundance of materials that can be used to create oversized, decorator-style clocks, including precut, round particleboard circles that come in up to 24-inch sizes. These circles can be embellished as gorgeous clocks for very little money. The other materials needed, with the exception of the clock mechanicals themselves, can also be purchased at these stores.

And for an even less expensive, slightly smaller clock, we used an old three-legged particleboard tabletop as the face for the music clock as seen above. Simply unscrew the legs of the table, remove the connecting brackets, and you have a ready-to-use 19-inch particleboard back you can embellish for a clock!)

MUSIC CLOCK: PREPARING THE TABLETOP

Remove all hardware from the back of an inexpensive, three-legged decorative table. If necessary, sand the edges of the circular tabletop with medium-grit sandpaper. Paint or spray paint the sides and outside edges of the tabletop black and let dry completely.

You will need to drill a hole in the exact center of your tabletop to accommodate the clock movement you have selected. (Our movement required a center hole 5/16 inch wide.)

1 To create a unique decorative edge on our music sheets, we used a safety lighter to lightly burn the edges of pieces of paper torn into random shapes, and then carefully extinguished the flame almost immediately. This project is not appropriate for children. If you wish to do this, you must be extremely careful, work over a heatproof surface, and burn only small areas of the paper at a time. Have a bucket of water nearby to extinguish any pieces of paper that burn too quickly. (We strongly recommend doing this over a kitchen sink half-filled with water, and that you wear a heatproof glove such as a heavy-duty oven mitt to hold the paper.) This step is not necessary to complete the clock, and you may skip it and proceed with the following steps if you wish.

Tear several old music sheets into large, random pieces.

2 Be sure your tabletop is clean and dust-free. Dry fit music sheets onto your clock face to ensure that you have a sufficient amount to cover the tabletop.

Pour a small amount of decoupage adhesive or thin wallpaper paste onto a disposable plate. Working on a protected surface covered with a drop cloth, carefully brush adhesive onto the back of the music sheet. Tip: Do not use newspaper to protect your work surface as the print will transfer to the music sheets.

Starting at the outer edge of the tabletop, glue music sheets into place in a random design. Use a slightly damp cloth or spatula to smooth out any air bubbles. Continue until you have covered the entire surface.

3 (Optional) You may wish to create a "center" for your clock using an appropriate graphic from an old music sheet cover or from a book. Cut out this decorative element and glue it to the center of the clock using the same process as Step 2. (Consider using a large music clef, one large music note, or an old 45 record.)

4 We found that most self-adhesive numbers designed for clocks came in either black or gold. You can create your own colors for these numbers if you wish, using either paint or other materials. We used a copper color to blend with the image in the center of our clock. We rubbed a copper finishing wax over the numbers and let it dry.

Insert the clock movement through the center of clock following directions. Place the clock number template guide over the stem of the movement, and use a ruler to locate the appropriate spot for each adhesive numeral.

Attach numbers, add heavy-duty picture hangers to the back of the clock, and hang.

Etched Window Frame

Turn a discarded window into an elegant display piece, for practically nothing.

To Make an Etched Window Frame You Will Need:

- A discarded, single-pane, multi-paneled glass window
- Work gloves
- Paint scraper
- Scissors
- Ruler
- Cardboard
- Masking tape (¼-inch, ½-inch)*
- Painter's tape (2-inch)
- Rubber gloves
- Etching cream**
- Plastic bag
- 1-inch foam brush
- Fabric (for background)
- Spray-on adhesive (we used 3M spray adhesive)***
- Utility knife
- Objects to be framed
- Standard screwdriver
- Hammer
- Glazier points****
- Picture hanging kit
- Window cleaner, paper towels

Optional Elements:
- Paint and paintbrush
- Fine sandpaper
- Wood putty and knife

* ¼-inch painter's tape is available at automotive supply stores.

** Glass etching cream is sold at craft or hobby stores under names such as Armour Etch, or it can be ordered from online sites such as www.joann.com.

***Spray adhesive is available at craft or hardware stores.

**** Glazier points are available at any hardware store.

Old window frames have a beauty all their own, even if their days as a functional home fixture have passed them by.

It's possible to give these old windows a second life as a decorative display piece with just a couple of hours of work, and a few dollars in materials. Better yet, once finished, these windows can spotlight favorite family photos, decorative cards, pressed flowers, or even to hold dainty ladies' handkerchiefs from days gone by.

For this project, we used an old basement window with three glass panes, but you can use any small multi-paneled window as long as the frame is solidly constructed. By applying glass etching cream to each of the panes, we were able to create a "frosted mat" to frame our photos. We covered the back of the window with a colorful fabric, attached hanging hardware, and finished the project in less than two hours.

Please note: Because the materials used for etching the glass are extremely caustic, follow all safety recommendations from the manufacturer exactly. And as a common-sense note, please remember that old windows—or glass of any kind—can be sharp, so wear gloves when handling the panes. It's also important to hang this window securely against a solid wall in an area where traffic is limited, so that family or friends won't bump into the piece.

SPECIAL TIP

Because our old, single-pane, three-frame window was relatively small and easy to handle, we left our glass panes in place when applying the etching cream. However, if your window has more than three panes, or if you would find it difficult to place the window into a sink to rinse off the etching cream, you can remove the individual glass panels following the instructions in Step 1 and etch each piece of glass following the remaining steps. Work on each pane on a flat, covered area, being careful to keep etching cream off your work surface.

You can then replace the etched panes before Step 11, and proceed with the project.

If you have never repaired an old window, it may be useful to know that single-glass panes are held into old window frames with small metal tips called glazier points. These small metal triangles are tapped into the frame sideways and then covered with window caulking to create a waterproof seal around the window. When you scrape old caulk away from the edge of the frame, you may run into these metal points every few inches. They can be pried out gently with the tip of a screwdriver to free the glass.

And remember: If the window frame you are using has a cracked pane or if you accidentally crack a pane during the project, you can have a new piece of window glass cut to fit that panel at any hardware store. Add the new pane to the frame by tapping in new glazier points along the wooden frame supports. Because we will be fitting a cardboard back onto the window in Step 11 for additional support, it is not necessary to replace the caulk.

1 Depending on the condition and overall look of your window, you may want to freshen up the frame with a coat of paint. Scrape away any loose paint and fill any gaping holes with wood putty. Using fine sandpaper, sand any rough edges or peeling paint. Paint the window with one coat of paint and let dry. (optional) Use fine-grade sandpaper to bring back some of the window's original distressed look.

2 Place the window frame flat on a firm surface. Remove any damaged window caulking from around all glass panes using a paint scraper. Work slowly and carefully. Don't press too hard on the glass or you may crack the pane. (We removed this caulk because it will show through the front of the window. If your panes are particularly loose after removing this old caulk, you can add additional glazier points to the frame to secure the window while you proceed with the next few steps.)

3 We decided to frame three 4-by-6-inch photos. To determine the shape of the etched matting we will create, we cut a 4-by-6-inch template out of cardboard to allow us to determine the position of the final photo in each pane.

4 Working from the back side of the window (where you removed the caulk), center the template on the glass in an attractive position and tape in place. This lets you visualize the size of the etched-glass "matting" you will need to create. (Note: Our individual window panes were 10-by-16 inches. These next few measurements are based on that. If your window size is different, you will need to experiment with individual "mat" sizes that look best in your window.)

After placing our template, we were left with 3 inches on each side of our window pane and 5 inches each on the top and bottom. We found that using ½-inch and 2-inch tape would create perfect symmetry around our print. Masking tape is used on the front side of the glass (where you will apply the etching cream) for two reasons: The first is to act as a guide to keep the lines of the etching straight and even. The second is to protect the part of the glass surface that you do not want etched. We used painter's tape (which is usually blue) on the back of our window because the difference in color shows exactly where we will apply our etching cream. The tape sizes you will need may vary depending on the size of your individual windows.

SPECIAL TIP

Work on preparing and etching only one glass pane at a time.

5 Working on the front side of the window, place ½-inch masking tape around the outside edge of the window. Be sure the edge of the tape is flush with the frame. This will prevent any etching cream from bleeding through.

6 On the back side of the window, we placed 2-inch painter's tape around the inside edge of the ½-inch masking tape. This 2-inch tape acts as a guide to keep the lines of the tape on the front of the window straight. Turn window over so the front faces up again.

7 You should now have a "frame" inside the blue painter's tape of clear glass visible from the front of your window pane. The etched portion of your frame will follow the outlines of the 2-inch piece of tape visible through the back of the frame.

Cut a piece of plastic from a plastic bag that is slightly smaller than the inside dimensions of the blue painter's tape and place the plastic over the cardboard template visible through the back of the exposed glass. Tape in place with 2-inch masking tape, using the inside edge of the blue tape on the back of the window as your guide. You should now have a 2-inch rectangle of glass exposed and ready for etching cream. Tip: To create clean lines, use a ruler as a guide to trim away ends of tape.

8 (Optional) Add a decorative detail to your matting by placing ¼-inch masking tape diagonally in all four corners. This step adds a nice decorative touch to the overall finished look.

9 Following manufacturer's directions exactly, brush etching cream over entire area of exposed glass. Always protect skin and eyes by wearing long sleeves, rubber gloves, and safety glasses, and work in a well-ventilated area close to a water source.

10 Rinse off etching cream thoroughly after time determined by manufacturer. Remove tape from window. Clean pane thoroughly. (Be sure to keep your rubber gloves on until all etching cream has been completely removed from the window.)

Repeat Steps 4 through 10 on remaining panes.

11 Cut a piece of cardboard to cover the glass for each windowpane. Note: Old windows are seldom exactly the same size from pane to pane. Cut each cardboard backing piece one at a time and test each for fit before proceeding.

Place cardboard over fabric and cut fabric about 1 inch larger than the cardboard. Press fabric to remove any wrinkles. Spray cardboard with a spray adhesive.

12 With adhesive side down, place cardboard in center of fabric and press in place. Turn cardboard over and smooth out fabric. Trim fabric, leaving ½ inch of material beyond edge of cardboard. (This will help cover any light gaps that may occur.) Tip: Be sure that your hands are free of any adhesive before touching the fabric, as the adhesive is not easily removed.

13 Center print on fabric-covered cardboard. Hold in place using double-sided tape. Place on window to ensure that the print is centered.

14 Using standard screwdriver and hammer, tap in glazier points to hold framed cardboard-backing in place. Make sure each pane fits securely into the window and that the individual panes do not shift. Attach appropriate hanging hardware to your window frame, and hang securely against a wall where the piece will not be bumped by passersby or children.

Classic Winter Potpourri

Mix cloved citrus fruit with other sweet-smelling items to make your house fragrant and delicious all season.

When outside doors close for the season, many of us turn to scented candles, potpourri, or other fragrant enhancers to make our homes smell as warm and wonderful as they feel. That's why the old-fashioned craft of cloved oranges should be a part of your activities this year. Cloved oranges are a key ingredient in a long-lasting potpourri basket that's perfect for making your house seem as though you've spent the day baking.

This simple technique works well with any citrus fruit, including lemons and limes. The mingled fragrance of the spicy cloves and the tart, clean citrus lasts almost indefinitely, making this a display for all the winter months.

You can stud an orange completely with cloves in the classic manner, or pierce it in fun patterns for a decorative look. Choose symmetrical fruit with even skin tones and no blotches or nicks. You can render a simple pattern on an orange in 30 to 45 minutes, but cloving a whole fruit takes longer.

To finish the potpourri basket, you'll need a small, low container and a few other items: Purchase whole cinnamon sticks at your local grocery or craft store. (Craft stores often have larger, more attractive sticks available in large bunches.) Pull out a few feet of colorful gingham ribbon and tie the cinnamon sticks together in batches of five or six. Another addition to this basket are pinecones that have been sprayed with vanilla room spray, or simply sprinkled with good household vanilla and left to dry. Pile each of these items in your basket and place on a dresser or tabletop, and you'll be rewarded with a heavenly scent all season long.

To Make a Decorative Clove Orange You Will Need:

- Whole cloves (available in the grocery department)
- Small- to medium-sized citrus
- Felt-tip pen
- A thimble OR ballpoint pen
- Sharp knife
- Wire and ribbon (optional)

SPECIAL TIP

If you want to hang your clove oranges, you can bend a thin piece of galvanized wire with a needle-nosed pliers into a "T" shape at one end.

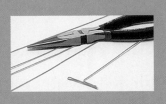

Thread the wire through the center of the baked and cooled oranges, letting the base of the fruit sit on the "T." Twist the top portion of the wire into a loop. Let the oranges finish drying by hanging them from the hook in a cool, dry, well-ventilated spot.

As an alternative, you can cut a piece of ribbon about 7 inches long, and then attach the ribbon to the fully dried orange using hot glue or by securing the ribbon in place with straight pins. Hot-glue a miniature pinecone over the head of the straight pins for an added decorative touch.

1 We decided to make clove oranges with a patterned design, and then to slice the fruit so that it split open into an attractive pattern while it dried.

Mark location of cloves with an erasable felt-tip pen. We found that the fruit dried best when the orange was divided lengthwise into eighths.

2 Insert the cloves along marked lines.

(If you find it difficult to push some of the cloves into the orange, lightly pierce the skin of the orange with a ballpoint pen first, then insert the clove. Or you can put a thimble on your finger and use that to push the clove into the fruit.)

3 Using a sharp knife, carefully cut just through the skin of the orange between the rows of the cloves starting about ½ inch from the top of the orange and stopping about the same distance from the bottom. Be careful not to cut too deeply into the fruit or it will cause the fruit to collapse during the drying process.

Dry fruit as noted in sidebar at right.

HOW TO DRY YOUR CLOVE ORANGES

There are several ways to dry clove oranges. The most traditional technique calls for treating the fruit with a substance called orris root, which prevents the fruit from molding as it air-dries. However, since this product may not be commonly available, we chose to dry our oranges in the oven.

Preheat your oven to 250°F. Place the oranges a few inches apart on wire baking racks, and place a foil-lined drip pan under the racks to catch the juice that will seep out as the oranges bake.

Our best results came from baking the oranges about 2½ hours, turning the fruit every 30 minutes or so. (Your cooking time may vary.) At the end of this time, the fruit will still be slightly soft. Line cooling racks with a double layer of paper towels, remove the oranges from the oven (they will be hot!), and place them on the racks to cool. Once the oranges are cool, place them in a cool, dry, well-ventilated spot to finish drying. It will take about one week for the fruit to completely harden.

Great Lamp Shades

Give ready-made lamp shades your creative touch and bring a new glow to your rooms.

After you've picked out your pillows and recovered your chaise, the only thing that remains is to cast the right light on them with the perfect lamp shade.

But don't be limited by the shades available in stores when you can use your imagination and some simple materials to create your own special look. Hand-crafted shades are fun to make and beautiful to look at, and you can customize them to complement any decor.

Our three unique shades here take from a few hours to a day to complete, including drying time. You can use our ideas to get started, or change the colors to fit your needs, experimenting with different papers, flowers, stencils, beads, tassels, and jewelry to create lamp shades that set just the right mood.

To Make a "Metallic" Lamp Shade You Will Need:

- ◆ Lamp shade
- ◆ Latex varnish
- ◆ Hair dryer (optional)
- ◆ Tissue paper
- ◆ Wallpaper paste (we used border adhesive)
- ◆ Various craft paints
- ◆ Plastic plates (for mixing paints)
- ◆ Pearl glaze
- ◆ Bronze glaze
- ◆ Latex glazing liquid
- ◆ Rags
- ◆ Paintbrush
- ◆ Rubber leaf stamps
- ◆ Acrylic metallic paints: copper, bronze, pearl
- ◆ Butterfly stencil
- ◆ Stencil brush or old, fairly stiff-bristled brush
- ◆ Artist brushes

1 Apply a coat of latex varnish to strengthen the surface of the shade. Allow to dry completely. Note: Since this lamp shade has several layers and shades of glaze on it, using a hair dryer to speed the drying process may be helpful.

2 Crumple tissue paper and tear into pieces that are each about 6 to 8 inches wide. Rip the edges of the paper so that they are uneven. Apply wallpaper paste to the shade in a small area, and lay a piece of tissue paper onto the pasted surface. Brush over it with more paste. Let about ½ inch of tissue paper extend over the top and bottom portion of the shade. (Wrinkles will occur as the paper is glued into place.) Continue around the shade until the entire surface is covered. Let dry.

3 When your shade has dried, trim the overlapping tissue paper edges and turn under, securing the tissue paper inside the shade with craft glue.

After edges have been glued, give the shade another coat of latex varnish. (You want to make the surface less absorbent so the glaze in Step 4 won't be quickly absorbed into the paper.) Allow to dry completely.

4 Mix about a tablespoon of white latex paint with a few drops of green craft paint, and then mix roughly 1 part combined paint to 3 parts untinted latex glazing liquid. Test your mixture on a sheet of paper to make sure it's translucent. (You want light to pass through the shade. If your glaze is too dense, add more glazing liquid.) Brush glaze onto shade and remove excess with a rag. Hold the shade up to a light while you work so you can see what it will look like when illuminated. Allow glaze to dry completely. When dry, apply a second coat of pearlized glaze over the first layer. This second coat will help your shade reflect light beautifully.

5 Decorate your shade with leaf stamps by applying paint to the stamp and pressing it onto the shade. It's okay if the impression is uneven because of the texture of the paper. You can fill in with your brush or leave it uneven, if you like. For your branches, connect the leaves with simple, slightly curved lines. (We used metallic bronze paint for the branches.)

We created a butterfly stencil by tracing a butterfly from a book and then transferring the drawing with carbon paper to cardboard. We cut out the shapes with an X-acto knife.

Using copper paint, we stenciled on the butterflies. You can use a proper stencil brush or, as we used here, an old artist's brush with fairly stiff bristles. Use very little paint (remove the excess by rubbing your brush on a piece of scratch paper before rubbing on the stencil.)

6 As a final coat, we applied a bronze glaze, mixed with a little untinted glaze to give us an antique patina. (You can make your own bronze glaze by using artist's acrylic bronze paint and diluting it with untinted latex glaze liquid.) Finish the edges of your shade with acrylic bronze paint, if you wish.

To Make a "Peony" Lamp Shade You Will Need:

- Lamp shade
- Rubber gloves
- Latex varnish
- Paintbrush
- Latex glazing liquid
- Latex paint
- Peony leaves*
- Spray paint (we used mocha brown)
- Plastic plates (for mixing paint)
- Rags

*This technique can be used with any type of fresh leaves or plant material. Other options might be fern fronds, ornamental grasses, or any other leaf with an interesting shape.

1 Put on rubber gloves. Paint shade with latex varnish and let dry completely. This provides a base on your shade.

2 To enhance our shade's appearance, we added a decorative glaze, made from glazing liquid and paint. We used a light-brown paint, and mixed it 1 part paint to 3 parts glaze liquid.

Rub the glaze on the shade in circular motions, and pat off excess with a rag to softly color the surface. Allow the glaze to dry.

3 Lay peony leaves on the shade as a stencil and spray over them lightly with your spray paint.

Let the paint come out in soft spritzes. This will give you a little more control than if the paint comes out too fast and forcefully. Shift the placement of leaves as you go around the shade until you get a pattern you find interesting. Here we went around the shade twice.

To Make a Fun Flower Shade You Will Need:

- Self-adhesive lamp shade*
- Rice paper**
- Scissors
- Craft glue
- Acrylic latex satin varnish
- Silk flowers
- Hot-glue gun
- Various craft paints: (green for the leaves and a contrasting color for highlighting leaves)
- Plastic plates (for mixing paint)
- Rubber leaf-shaped stamps
- Artist brushes
- Craft adhesive
- Chandelier crystals
- Thumbtack
- **Optional:** Beading headpins, pearl studs, earring backs (all are available where beading supplies are sold)

*These shades have an adhesive material on the shade form, covered by a protective plastic that must be removed. These shades are available at fabric or craft stores.

**Rice paper is available at art supply or craft stores.

1 Remove the protective paper from the lamp shade. Set lamp shade aside for the moment.

Using the protective paper as a pattern, cut your rice paper about 1 inch larger than the pattern.

2 Line up your shade with the rice paper pattern, leaving ½ inch of excess at both the top and bottom. Carefully roll your shade onto the rice paper and smooth the paper onto the adhesive portion of the shade. Don't worry if there are some wrinkles—it adds to the effect.

Trim the edges and smooth the excess paper under the rim, securing with craft glue. Apply a coat of latex varnish to the entire shade to give your paper a strong finish. Allow to dry completely. (You can speed drying of your varnish by using a hairdryer.)

3 Clip the heads off a variety of silk flowers. Attach flower heads to the shade using a drop of hot glue.

4 Apply paint to your leaf stamp and press stamp onto the shade around the flowers. Vary the number of leaves per flower from one to three. Use an artist brush to highlight the leaves with small lines of lighter or brighter color. (We used a turquoise blue-green.)

5 As a further embellishment, we secured pearl studs strung on thin wire headpins (available from stores that sell beading supplies) to the shade using earring backs.

Slide a pearl onto a headpin and secure with a drop of craft adhesive. Use a thumbtack to gently poke a hole in the shade where you want the pearl. Slide headpin through the hole. Place a dab of craft cement on an earring back and then slide the back over the headpin inside the shade to hold the pin in place. Clip off any excess wire from the headpin.

6 To finish, use a thumbtack to poke regularly spaced holes along the bottom edge of the shade. Use these holes to hang vintage chandelier crystals. (You could also finish the bottom of your shade with fringe or beaded trim.)

Old-Fashioned Runner

This super-simple technique lets you turn scraps of old fabric into a variety of colorful and clever items.

This project is a simple—and addictive!—way to transform small pieces of old fabric into a wide variety of decorative pieces.

You can use this technique to make table runners, pillow covers, and even bedspreads with a delightful mix-and-match of colors and prints. Best of all, this technique is a perfect way to create something beautiful without spending a great deal of time on the project. You can create these fabric circles while you're watching television, or simply relaxing, and before you know it, you'll have enough for any decorative object you want. You'll even find this project perfect for kids who are old enough to use very simple sewing skills.

To Make a Simple Old-Fashioned Runner You Will Need:

◆ Lightweight cotton fabric remnants
◆ Small bowl (for tracing circle outlines)*
◆ Fabric marking pencil
◆ Scissors
◆ Needle and thread
◆ Iron

*The size bowl you select will determine the finished size of the fabric circle you create. We used a bowl that was about 6 inches in diameter. Experiment to find the perfect size for your project.

SPECIAL TIP

Use fabrics of the same weight in order to keep size of your circles consistent.

1 Trace circles on wrong side of fabric and cut. (The number of circles required will depend on the finished item you intend to create.) Test two or more sizes before cutting all your fabric remnants.

2 With wrong side of fabric facing down, turn ¼ inch of raw edge of fabric toward center of the circle. Using a double-threaded needle, run a gathering stitch around the entire circle. (A gathering stitch is simply a series of small, neat stitches used when gathering cloth by hand.)

Knot the thread at one end to keep your thread from slipping while sewing. Turn the fabric edge as you sew your gathering stitch.

3 Pull gently on ends of threads to form gathers. Tie several knots to secure gathers. Cut away thread. Press flat with iron.

4 With gathered sides of circles facing in, attach circles together using an overcast stitch. The amount of stitching required is about ½ to ¾ inch.

5 When attaching the fabric circles together, we suggest that you make a series of single vertical or horizontal rows, and then attach the rows together. This will help to keep the grouping of the circles square.

Heirloom Ornaments

Add some sparkle to your life with these fun ornaments.

Take a peek into any box of treasured holiday decorations, and you'll probably find a special sequined ornament, perhaps made during the 1950s or 1960s by someone in your family.

Sequined ornaments were something of a craze during that time. Each ball was carefully hand-decorated using straight pins and tiny sequins to catch and reflect the light. Today, these old-fashioned favorites can be updated using new materials readily available in any fabric or craft store to both provide you with a relaxing project, and to add a handmade touch to any holiday decorating. Tiny seed pearl beads, ready-made sequined cord, colorful satin ribbons, and a variety of other decorative beading supplies can all contribute to a one-of-a-kind decoration. In this case, we also found a way to speed up the process of making these unique ornaments by first covering our balls with ribbon, and then simply highlighting them with sequins and beads.

Best of all, these items make gifts that will be treasured by their recipient for years to come.

To Make an Heirloom Ornament You Will Need:

- ◆ Plastic foam balls in a variety of shapes and sizes
- ◆ Standard straight pins
- ◆ Assortment of ribbons and trims in a variety of colors and widths
- ◆ Craft scissors
- ◆ Assortment of sequins and beads in a variety of colors and styles
- ◆ Pearlized straight pins
- ◆ Hot-glue gun

1 Insert two straight pins into a plastic foam ball on opposite ends (at the axis points). Spin the ball gently while holding both pins to make sure that the pins are exactly opposite each other.

Beginning at one pin, wrap the ball with ribbon, going around the first pin, and then down the ball and around the other pin. Twist the ribbon each time you reach a pin and continue until you have covered the entire ball, slightly overlapping the ribbon edges. (We used ¾-inch ribbon for this ball.)

2 After the ball is completely covered, use your pins to secure the ribbon at each end and cut, keeping the end of the ribbon close to the pin. Add a second layer of ribbon in a coordinating color by inserting a pin through the ribbon at one of the axis points. (We used a second piece of ribbon to divide the ball into quarters.)

3 Cut the second ribbon, keeping the end close to the pin. You can add additional ribbons by following the previous steps, varying the design and colors you want. Tip: Working with satin ribbons can be a little tricky since they tend to be slippery. Don't be afraid to use additional pins to help keep the ribbon in place while wrapping the ball.

MAKE A CLASSIC SEQUINED ORNAMENT

Fully sequined ornaments are a bit more time-consuming to make than a ball that is first covered with ribbon and then simply embellished with sequins or decorative beads. However, the finished look is certainly worth the extra effort.

Draw a design on a foam ball using a felt-tip pen. It can be a bell, holly leaves, or even a simple geometric design. Decide which color sequin will be the overall color of your ornament, and then choose one or two contrasting-color sequins to highlight your design.

Pins come in a variety of lengths. Longer silk or pleat pins work best to attach heavier beads and applique pins are perfect for the sequins. (This is important on smaller balls where the pins begin to compete for space.) Choose a pin and a single sequin or bead and place inside your pattern. Add a small bead or pearl between the sequin and the pin for more dimension.

You may want to experiment by using readymade sequined "rope" to mimic this technique more quickly. This product, available in fabric stores, has many sequins sewn together in a row, one sequin wide. Use this flexible material to wrap a plastic foam ball as we did with the ribbon ornaments.

4 Once you've covered your foam ball with ribbon, embellish it further by using a variety of beads, sequins, and pearlized straight pins. Tip: To ensure that your decorative pins and beads will be evenly spaced, find the center point between the two axis points. Start inserting the pins and beads from the center, working out to the axis points.

5 To add additional texture to your ornament, wrap decorative trim around the center of the ball and secure in place with additional pins and beads.

SPECIAL TIPS

For safety's sake, since these ornaments do use a lot of pins and small beads, make sure the ornaments are displayed where children or pets won't have access to them.

To create a hanger for your ornament, cut a piece of ribbon about 8 inches long. Make a loop with the ribbon, and attach the loop at one of the axis points. Secure in place using pearlized pins.

No-Sew Throw

Use brightly-colored fleece to create this cuddly, no-sew blanket in less than an hour.

It's hard to beat the pleasure of a snuggly blanket on a cool evening. This incredibly easy, oh-so-soft throw is perfect for a leisurely nap or for cuddling under while watching television. Better yet, this simple, no-sew project can be completed in less than an hour, for less than $30 in materials.

The secret to this simple, colorful throw is a material called polar fleece, available in any fabric store. This supersoft product is easy to work with and, when cut, will not ravel at the edges. That makes it ideal for a no-sew project that can be completed in a snap—literally—since the edges of the blanket are secured with simple snap-on grommets.

Fleece comes in a wide variety of eye-catching colors and patterns. You can create the throw in matching shades, or choose two unique patterns to make it a reversible blanket. The choice is yours.

A couple of final hints: It's helpful to have a large, flat working surface when making these blankets. If you do not have a table big enough to spread the fabric out flat, work on a clean floor. Also, we used a type of snap-together plastic grommet to make our edging for these throws. You may find these at your local home improvement store, but if you can't locate them, any fabric or sewing store offers a wide variety of metal grommets that can be applied with a special tool that squeezes them together.

To Make a No-Sew Throw You Will Need:

◆ 4 yards of 60-inch polar fleece (2 yards each for front and back)
◆ Pins
◆ Scissors
◆ Measuring tape
◆ Plastic snap-together grommets*

*A wide variety of grommets are available at fabric and sewing stores. Traditional grommets come in two pieces and are snapped through fabric using a special tool. Another type of grommet is made of plastic and can be pressed together using your fingers. Either style works fine for this blanket.

1 Place both pieces of polar fleece fabric together, squaring the edges. Pin the layers of fabric together to keep them square. Use a sharp scissors to cut through both layers of fleece, leaving a 56-inch square. (Note: Save the leftover fabric for use in making the fringe in Step 3.)

2 Working on a flat surface, with both layers of fabric together, mark the placement of the grommets with pins every 3 to 4 inches apart along all four sides of the blanket. Use the tip of your scissors to cut a small hole for your first grommet about 1 inch from outside edge. Push the face of the grommet (the one with the stem) through the hole in the blanket. Snap the back of the grommet in place from the opposite side of the blanket. Repeat until you have placed all grommets.

3 We added a decorative fringe to our throw using a small piece of multicolored fleece threaded through each grommet.

To do this, cut 1-inch wide strips of polar fleece about 6 to 8 inches long. Fold strip in half and thread the looped end through the grommet. Pull the tails through the loop and tighten securely, creating a knot. After all the ties have been attached, trim them to a uniform length.

SPECIAL TIP

As an alternative to adding fringe to your throw, you can create a laced edge using the grommets. To do this, cut 1-inch wide strips of polar fleece 72 inches long. Lace the strip of fabric through the grommets, leaving tails on each corner. When all four sides are laced, tie the tails at the corners in a knot or bow. (Note: If this throw will be used by a child, we recommend stitching through this long piece of lacing into the blanket itself so that the child cannot remove the fleece strip, which could pose a choking hazard.)

Fun Board Games

These colorful, fun game boards make wonderful stocking stuffers, or unique table decorations for a holiday dinner.

Simple, old-fashioned board games are perennial favorites among kids both old and young. With these simple instructions, you can create a couple of different games either for gift-giving (try them as a stocking stuffer) or for a unique ice-breaker at the holiday dinner table. Set one game between every two place settings and let the diners compete for small holiday favors that you provide.

With the first traditional game, the peg jump, the object is to leave only one peg standing. Use a peg to jump over another into an empty hole. Remove the jumped peg. Continue until there are no jumps left to make.

Play by yourself or take turns with a partner. The player with most "captured" pegs when there are no moves remaining is the winner.

With tic-tac-toe, the winner has the added benefit of being able to eat or share the chocolate game pieces!

Either game makes a wonderful keepsake for guests to take home.

To Create a Fun Board Game You Will Need:

For Tic-Tac-Toe
- ◆ Four 1-inch ball feet
- ◆ 5-inch square wood plaque
- ◆ Candy (We used Hershey's Almond Kisses and Rolo caramels)

For Peg Jump
- ◆ 5-inch round wood plaque
- ◆ Three 1-inch ball feet
- ◆ Paper for pattern
- ◆ Pen
- ◆ Drill with ³⁄₁₆-inch bit
- ◆ 14 wooden golf tees

For both games
- ◆ 150-grit sandpaper
- ◆ Clear adhesive (we used Elmer's Household Cement)
- ◆ Acrylic craft paint (we used Americana Country Red, Lamp Black and Leaf Green)
- ◆ Art brushes
- ◆ White magic marker or pen
- ◆ Ruler
- ◆ Gold metallic craft paint (we used Dazzling Metallics "Glorious Gold")
- ◆ Masking tape
- ◆ Old newspaper
- ◆ Krylon 18KT. gold leafing pen*
- ◆ Krylon-brand Webbing spray in Gold Chiffon*

* These specialty products are available in craft or art supply stores.

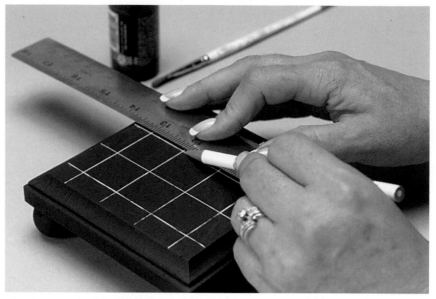

1 Using 150-grit sandpaper, sand any rough areas of both plaques. Wipe off dust. Then use clear adhesive to glue the ball feet to the bottom of the square plaque ½ inch in from each corner. On the round plaque, glue three ball feet, one at each corner of an imaginary triangle, ½ inch in from the edge of the plaque. Let glue dry for at least 30 minutes.

2 Set aside the round plaque for the moment. Paint the square plaque and feet black with craft paint. Allow the paint to dry. After the first coat has dried, lightly sand the plaque to remove raised grain. Wipe off the dust and apply a second coat of paint. Allow the paint to dry.

Once the second coat of paint has dried, you're ready to create the game surface. Using a white pencil or magic marker and a ruler, measure ½ inch in from each side of the plaque and draw four lines. Measure in another inch from each line and draw a second set of four lines. This will give you a border row of rectangles (squares in the corners) on the top of the plaque and nine 1-inch squares in the center.

3 Paint the center rectangle on each side of the border and the corner squares green. Paint the remaining rectangles on the border red. The black squares in the center will remain black.

Leave the curved edge that slants down from the top black. Paint the lower portion of the plaque gold.

4 Trace over the white lines on the top of the plaque with the Gold Leafing Pen. Also draw a line around the outside edge on the top of the plaque. Set the square plaque aside for the moment.

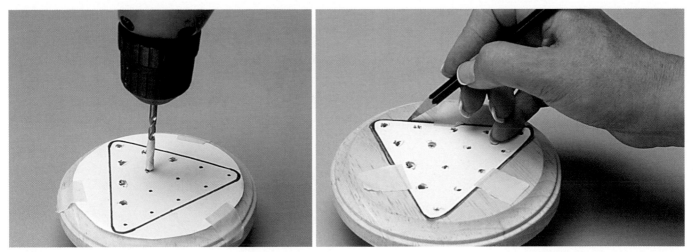

5 Return to the circular plaque for the peg jump game. Cut a circle of paper to fit on the top of the circular plaque. Using a pen, draw a triangle in the center of the paper.

Measure in about ¼ inch from each side of the triangle and mark with a dot where you will place your pegs. (Each side has five spaces for pegs, with an additional three spots in the center of the pattern.) Alternately, you can start at the top of one point of the triangle and create horizontal rows that have equal spaces marked: 1 dot for the first row, 2 dots for the second, and so on, until your final row at the bottom of the paper has 5 dots for pegs.)

Tape the pattern to the top of the plaque.

Wrap a piece of tape around the drill bit, ½ inch from the tip. (This will help get a consistent depth for each hole.) Drill the holes where indicated, going only as deep as the bottom of the tape.

Remove the pattern and set aside. The holes can be sanded by rolling a small piece of sandpaper into a tube. Insert the tube into the holes and twist. After sanding, cut out the triangular portion of your pattern along the triangle lines and replace over plaque. Trace around pattern. Paint the entire plaque black, but leave the pencil marks for your triangle unpainted as a guide for the next step.

6 Trace over the triangle's lines on the top of the plaque with the Gold Leafing Pen. Also draw a gold line around the outside edge on the top of the plaque.

Paint the area surrounding the triangle green. Paint the curved edge that slants down from the top red. Paint the edge of the plaque gold. Leave the interior of the triangle black.

7 Wrap a piece of masking tape around the edge and feet of both plaques to protect them from the webbing spray.

Shake the can of gold webbing well. (It's a good idea to practice spraying this sticky gold webbing material on a piece of newspaper first to give yourself an idea of how best to apply the product in a smooth manner.)

Once you're comfortable with your results, spray the webbing on both game boards.

To finish your peg jump game, lightly sand golf tees to remove any gloss and paint tees gold. Place painted pegs gently in the game holes to dry. To finish the tic-tac-toe game, add a small bag of candy to the board, with two different shapes to represent "x"s and "o"s.

Snow Dolls

A cute snow doll is a clever way to display outgrown toddler clothes!

You can get a lot of satisfaction from giving a gift custom-made for the recipient.

Here is an easy project for your Christmas and winter decor that you can really personalize, for yourself or as a gift. This adorable snowman is dressed in real kids' clothes! Do you have a special sweater or a precious pair of shoes from your child's (or grandchild's) toddler days? Use them to dress up this snowman and you'll have a family heirloom. If you start making them for gifts, you'll probably have to start shopping thrift stores, garage sales, or consignment stores for more doll clothes! In any event, this snow doll is guaranteed to melt hearts.

To Create a Snow Doll You Will Need:

For the body
- ½ yard white/cream felt (72 inches wide on bolt)
- 1 20-ounce bag polyester fiberfill
- Medium-weight white thread
- Pins
- Craft needles
- Scissors

For the face
- Eyes: 2 black buttons

- Nose: 1 small square orange felt
- Mouth: Black embroidery floss or permanent felt-tip pen
- Cheeks: Rose-toned blush make-up

For the clothing
- Child's cap
- Child's sweater or shirt
- Scarf
- Child's mittens/gloves
- Child's socks and shoes or boots

SNOW DOLL PATTERN (1 SQUARE = 1")

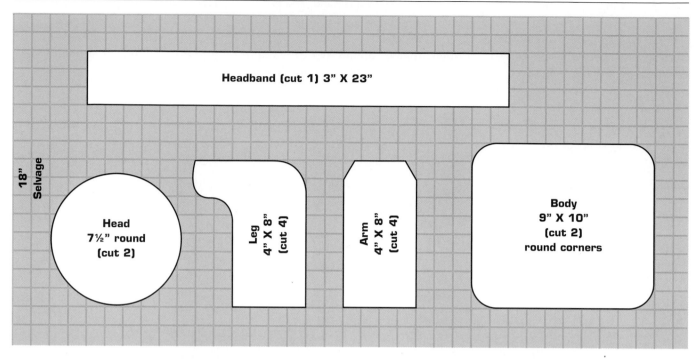

Headband (cut 1) 3" X 23"

18" Selvage

Head
7½" round
(cut 2)

Leg
4" X 8"
(cut 4)

Arm
4" X 8"
(cut 4)

Body
9" X 10"
(cut 2)
round corners

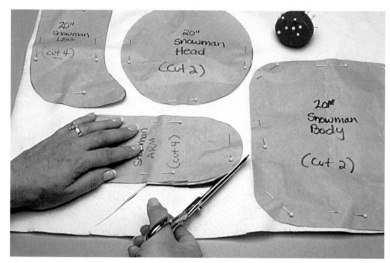

1 Precise pattern pieces aren't really necessary for this doll, as long as the arms and legs are proportionate in size to the head and body. With the dimensions shown here, your snow doll will be about 20 inches tall. You can adjust the pattern to make a smaller or bigger snowman, depending on the clothing you want to use. See Step 11 to help visualize how the stuffed doll will look.

For our dolls, we cut two circular head pieces about 7½ inches in diameter. The headband used to sew these together (cut one) was 23 inches long and 3 inches wide. Our arms (cut four) were roughly 8 inches long and 4 inches wide. The leg pattern pieces should resemble a Christmas stocking, with a "foot" at the end. These legs (cut four) were 8 inches long and 4 inches wide at the foot, narrowing down to about 3 inches long on the leg. Our body pieces (cut two) were rough oblongs that were 10 inches long and 9 inches wide, rounded at the corners.

Draw your pattern on a piece of paper. Pin pattern pieces on white/cream felt and cut.

2 Using ½-inch seam allowance, sew arm and leg pattern pieces together, leaving straight edge open to allow for stuffing of fiberfill. Sew the front and back of body pattern pieces together, leaving a 4-inch opening for stuffing.

NOTE

The body has rounded corners; the arms have rounded corners on the hand-end; the legs have rounded corners on the back ankle, top of toes and front ankle.

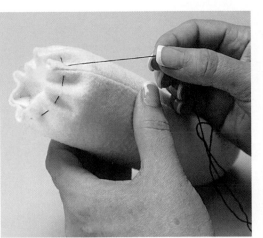

3 Turn the arms, legs, and body right-side out. Fill all five pieces firmly with fiberfill. (You can use a piece of dowel, a ruler, or a stick to pack the fiberfill firmly.)

4 Using a double-threaded needle, sew a basting stitch about ½ inch from the edge of the opening for the arms and legs. Pull on the thread to close the opening and double-knot to hold in place.

To close the opening on the body, turn in the edge of the opening ½ inch and hand stitch opening closed using a double-threaded needle.

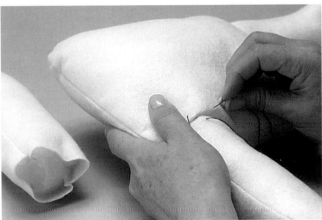

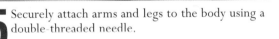

5 Securely attach arms and legs to the body using a double-threaded needle.

6 To make the head, sew the ends of the headband pattern piece together using a ½-inch seam allowance. You should now have a round circle of fabric.

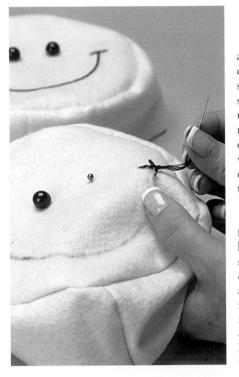

7 Pin headband to one side of the head pattern piece. Using ½-inch seam allowance, sew in place. Tip: Before you pin the first side of the head to the headband, fold both pieces in half and mark with pins. Then fold in half again and mark with pins. Line up the pins, secure in place, and sew.

Move to Step 8 and complete the facial features of the snowman before attaching the back of the head to the headband.

8 With the headband seam at the top of the head, lay out the location of the eyes, nose, and mouth using pins, taking into consideration the style of hat and scarf you will be using to dress your snow doll. Sew button eyes in place using a double-threaded needle. The mouth can either be embroidered or drawn on with a felt-tip pen. If you want to embroider the mouth, use a chain stitch with a minimum of three strands of embroidery floss.

Once you have completed the facial features, sew the back of the head to headband using ½-inch seam allowance. Leave a 3-inch opening through which you will add the stuffing. Turn the head right-side out and fill the head firmly with fiberfill. Turn in the edge of the opening ½ inch and hand stitch closed using a double-threaded needle.

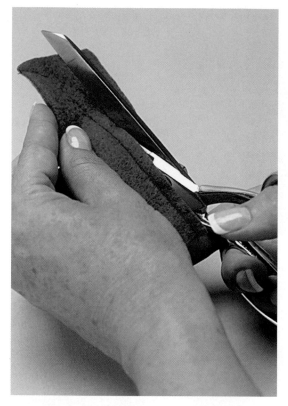

9 You don't need a pattern for the snow doll's carrot nose. It can be short and fat or long and skinny. The choice is yours.

To create the nose, fold the orange felt in half lengthwise. Using a felt-tip pen or pins, draw out the design of the nose, allowing extra material for a ½-inch seam allowance. Sew along markings, leaving an opening on the end to allow for stuffing. Trim away extra fabric; turn right-side out, and firmly stuff with fiberfill.

10 Using a double-threaded needle, run a basting stitch about ¼ inch from the edge of opening. Draw thread to close opening and double-knot to hold in place. (See Step 4 for help with this if needed.) Attach nose to face using a double-threaded needle.

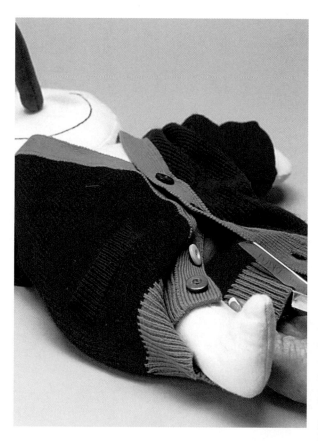

12 You will need to create leg openings in the sweater or shirt you have chosen for your snowman. If you are using a button-down sweater or shirt, unbutton it to the top of the legs of the snowman. Cut the back of the sweater or shirt to the top of the snowman's legs.

If your sweater or shirt is not a button-down, mark the location of the top of the snow-man's legs with a pin and cut through both sides of the garment up to the pin. Remove the

11 Securely attach the head to the body of the snowman using a double-threaded needle. Be sure to run your stitches around the front and back of the head.

sweater or shirt, turn the garment wrong-side out and sew the leg openings closed, either by machine or by hand. Your stitching line should appear "U-shaped." Finish dressing your snow doll with hat, mittens, scarf, and shoes.

Add a little to blush to the cheeks and your doll is complete.

MAKE A SNOW DOLL DOOR TOPPER

As a variation on the snow doll itself, create a clever door topper by following some of the same steps shown previously to create a head for the snow doll, and then attaching it to a wooden back.

To Make a Snow Doll Door Topper You Will Need:

- One unstuffed head, created using previous directions
- A piece of scrap wood, about 4 by 7 inches
- Two long twigs (for arms)
- Wood glue or hot glue
- Heavy-duty stapler or small nails (brads)
- Picture-hanger hardware
- Scarf and hat

1 Attach the picture-hanger hardware at the top center of the piece of wood.

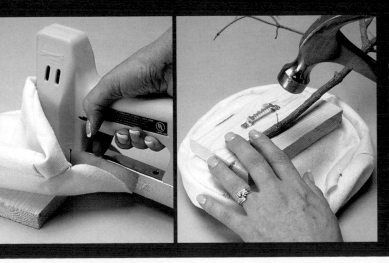

2 Turn wood over so that the picture-hanger hardware is on the back of the plaque. Turn the empty snowman head inside out, and staple to the top and middle of the front of the piece of wood. Turn head right-side out, fill with polyfill, and hand stitch closed.

Then, using hot glue or wood glue, attach the twigs to the board to serve as arms for your door topper. You may also want to staple or nail the twigs to the wood for more stability. Handsew the stocking cap to the head, tie a scarf around the top and the sides of the piece of wood, and tie it in front.

Chapter

two

Transformation

Don't throw it out, or pay good money to get it fixed. Transform it—all by yourself—into something new and beautiful!

Quick Furniture Fixes

Caring for and cleaning wood furniture doesn't have to be a chore. In fact, these simple tips can save you time and money.

It's inevitable. No matter how hard you try to avoid it, either you, someone in your family, or even a friend is going to do a number on a piece of your beautiful wood furniture. You'll gasp at this terrible scrape, scratch, dent, chip, or smear. Now what?

Furniture suffers abuse every day. People. Pets. Sunlight. Moisture. Food. They all take their toll.

We could go on, listing mishap after mishap, because co-existing with kids, dogs, cats, a husband, a huge living room picture window with a west view and other dangers, aren't kind to furniture.

Luckily, there are some general care and quick-fix tricks to help keep your furniture looking beautiful.

Finessing Finishes

When you clean a piece of furniture, remember that you are actually cleaning the finish on the piece, and not the wood itself. In some cases, particularly if the piece has been polished repeatedly over the course of a number of years, you may actually be cleaning only the wax on top of your finish. (See below.)

In general, there are three types of finishes—hard, soft, and painted—that were used to seal and protect the bare wood when the piece of furniture was made.

Hard finishes are most common. These clear, often "shiny" or "glossy" finishes include shellac, varnish, lacquer, and polyurethane. Sometimes it's easy to tell a hard finish, particularly on an older piece of furniture covered with a varnish, because the surface will begin to yellow or "alligator"—that is, to display a variety of cracks and lines running through the finish itself.

The second type of finish, sometimes found on handmade furniture items, is called a soft finish. These pieces have been "sealed" by repeated buffing with oil or wax, and they may have a matte-looking surface, rather than an extremely shiny one. Painted finishes are self-explanatory.

If you don't know which type of finish your wood originally had, there are a few simple tests you can do. This can be helpful if you decide to strip off the old finish to refinish the piece so that you can select the correct

If you suspect your furniture has a "soft" finish comprised of linseed oil, dribble a few drops on an inconspicuous spot to test.

product or technique for doing so. (For instance, hard finishes will generally require a mineral spirit-based refinishing product.)

If you suspect your wood has a hard finish (shellac, varnish, lacquer, or polyurethane), test the material in an inconspicuous spot this way: Take a small amount of acetone (or an acetone-based fingernail polish remover), and rub the acetone gently into a small area of the finish. This test is damaging to the finish, so test on a spot that cannot be seen.

If your finish is lacquer, it will liquefy about 30 seconds after applying the acetone. If it's varnish or shellac, the finish will become sticky after about 90 seconds and the surface will look sort of the way that fingernail polish does when it's being removed. If the finish on your wood is polyurethane, the acetone will roll around like water off a duck's back.

If you suspect that a piece of furniture in your house has a soft finish, try drizzling a small amount of boiled linseed oil (available at any hardware store) onto a small, finished area. Again, remember to do this test in an inconspicuous spot. Rub the oil gently onto the surface. If the wood sucks up the linseed oil, you have an oil finish. If it beads up on the surface, you probably have a hard finish.

Whatever your finish, if your piece of furniture feels at all gummy or looks dull, it may have a buildup of cleaning products on it, rather than a poor finish. This is a problem particularly if you have switched polishes over the years, or if the wood has been exposed to a high concentration of body oils and perfumes.

To clean off old wax or other surface spoilers, try washing the piece with a mild detergent and water solution first. According to www.furniturefixer.com

(a Web site that specializes in mail-order furniture-care items and restoration), proceed cautiously, making certain that the cleaning solution does not affect anything more than the wax and dirt buildup. If the piece is severely soiled, you may want to consult a professional for advice.

Cleaning Tips

For any finish, it's best to dust your piece carefully with a soft, clean rag that has been slightly dampened—only wet enough to pick up the dirt, but not enough to actually moisten the wood, suggests Charles Sutton, president of Sutton House Furniture, a designer and consultant for fine furniture manufacturers. And while you may like using a feather duster, don't use it on wood. Dusters simply redistribute grit and soil, and using one can scratch your piece with an errant quill. Finally, lift objects off your furniture, rather than sliding them from side to side, which can catch grit underneath the object and possibly scratch the piece.

Dust your furniture all you like, but polish it with your favorite liquid or paste wax only three to four times per year, unless the piece is frequently used, suggests Sutton. And as for choosing an everyday cleaner, read the label. That should explain whether the product is best suited for your finish.

Hard On Your Furniture?

I have a coffee table with a hard polyurethane finish that suffered the indignity of one too many gouges from my infant daughter's rolling chair. The black skid marks on the legs of that table were truly wicked.

Since my everyday cleaner wasn't removing those marks, I turned to Jamie Gibbs, principal of Jamie Gibbs & Associates, an interior design and architectural firm in New York City. Gibbs has been in the design business for more than 25 years and frequently advises clients on how to best care for their antiques. He directed me to my nearest upscale grocery store to

Lemon oil and mayonnaise removes wax and dirt buildup. Butcher's wax seals up the beauty.

pick up a few items: lemon oil, Butcher's Wax … and something I already had on hand. Mayonnaise.

Lemon oil, as the name indicates, is a byproduct of that citrus frequently used for cleaning and caring for quality wood furniture. Butcher's Wax is a clear paste wax originally developed in 1880. It is used for, among other things, cleaning and protecting bowling alley lanes, but like other paste waxes, it also works well to polish, preserve, and protect fine wood. As for the mayonnaise, well, that's usually used for salads, but in this case, it provides cleaning power as well.

"Start with a teaspoon or two of lemon oil and mayonnaise to remove wax and dirt buildup," Gibbs suggests. Scour the area very gently with a soft rag or, for harder-to-remove blights, use a very fine stainless steel pad to help with the cleaning process.

"After removing all the excess crud, wipe the furniture with lemon or cottonseed oil and let it sit," he says. "After a few hours, polish the furniture with a lint-free rag to remove excess oil and brighten the finish. Lastly, apply Butcher's Wax."

I have to say, the unusual combination worked like a charm, except that I had to keep pushing the dog away from the mayonnaise-laced areas. Grrr.

Remember, too, Gibbs says, that many of the marks you find on your furniture—water marks, small scratches, and such—might actually be in the wax on your wood, not in the finish. A quick fix for some prob-

lems can be to either place a thick rag over the stain and press with a warm iron (the heat will lift the stain off the wax), or to strip the wax and reapply.

Quick Fix-Its

If you're faced with blemishes on your furniture, you may wonder if you can handle the problem on your own. "It depends," says Gibbs. "Ink stains on unsealed wood, grease stains, and, of course, extensive damage to varnish or lacquer require the services of an expert." But there are some things you can try at home. Here are some handy tips:

Small scratches will often disappear when rubbed carefully with furniture polish or paste wax. If that doesn't work, try using a nut meat. Need to erase that scratch in your walnut tabletop? Crack a walnut shell and rub the oily, meaty nut carefully into the scratch, trying not to touch the surrounding area. After filling in the abrasion, carefully dab polish on the area.

Marking pens are another quick fix for dings, scratches, and other little problems with your wood furniture. Head to your nearest art supply store, where you'll find not only brown and black markers, but also all those terrific in-between colors, such as red-brown (for cherry furniture), golden brown (for maple), and dark brown (for walnut).

Swipe the pen over the scratch and then quickly wipe off the excess with a tissue—or better yet, your index finger. If the repair color is too light, you can apply a second coat. The color only has to be close to disappear.

Marking pens provide an instant and excellent touch-up for small scratches and discolorations.

Finally, shoe polish (wax, not liquid) works better on areas where a larger application around intricate carvings or scroll work is needed. Rub it on as you would on your shoes, then buff it off. It's easy, but as with other quick fixes, the color may come off with regular cleaning and need to be reapplied.

A combination of baking soda and mineral oil may be the ticket for removing a small burn that has not penetrated the finish. Mix the two and gently rub the area in the same direction as the grain. If you're not up to stripping and reapplying wax, you can fill the indentation with clear fingernail polish, let it dry, then polish the whole area to a glossy sheen. This combination of baking soda and oil will also work on small stains.

Furniture is made to be used, enjoyed, and handed down to those who think of it in sentimental terms. Take care of your special pieces, and you will be rewarded with decades of enjoyment.

Shoe polish in a matching color can provide an easy touch-up for marred furniture. Simply wipe on and wipe off completely.

To Fix a Dog-Chewed Chair Leg You Will Need:

◆ The damaged chair*
◆ A plastic drop cloth
◆ Masking tape
◆ Fine- and medium-grit sandpaper
◆ Putty knife
◆ Wood putty
◆ Primer
◆ Paint or clear sealant

*This process works on painted finish chairs. However, this technique will also work on wooden chair legs with a natural finish. Strip off any hard finish on the leg before starting the process, using a product designed for that use, following manufacturer's directions. Then select a wood putty in a color that matches the chair leg, and fill any scratches or gouges. Once the holes have been filled, refinish the leg with polyurethane or varnish to cover the fix.

1 To protect the surface of your chair or other furniture piece, wrap the body of the item in a plastic drop cloth and tape securely.

2 Use a medium-grit sandpaper to lightly sand the entire leg or other damaged area on the chair. You want to smooth any rough spots from the wood before proceeding.

3 Use a putty knife to carefully smooth wood putty into all gouges and other scratches on the leg. Try to keep the material flat against the chair leg, and use a gentle pressure on the putty knife to force material into the holes. Let dry thoroughly.

4 Use fine-grain sandpaper to smooth the dried wood putty until the surface feels smooth against your hand and then prime the chair leg. I applied two light coats of primer, sanding lightly after each coat.

5 Paint each leg of the chair at the same time to balance and refresh. Allow to dry.

Home as Art

Cheryl Natt views her home as a canvas, using color, collections, and charm to create a space that centers around having fun at home.

Before

Welcome Home

To step into freelance artist Cheryl Natt's home is to be engulfed in a fruit bowl of color, swept away in a riot of shades that include raspberry-reds, cool cantaloupe yellows, and bold stripes of grape-green.

In fact, in recent years, Natt has seldom met a surface that she didn't feel was improved by a bold blast of color. She confesses that in the nine years she and her husband Mike have lived in their two-story home, she's painted and repainted 26 times.

You could say that Natt views anything approaching the "status quo" in her home with suspicion. A room is never "done," and a collection of clever, funky, and fun items is never so complete that another newcomer can't be made welcome.

Take Buck, a stuffed, life-sized toy dog that she found for a dollar on one of her many garage sale outings. She snatched it up and brought it home, where it was greeted initially with a thorough sniffing by her Shar Pei puppy, Valentine. Convinced that the interloper wouldn't be sampling her food dish, Valentine quickly lost interest, but Natt didn't. The toy dog began to make periodic appearances throughout the house, dressed in a variety of fashions, usually placed in a spot designed to surprise her (according to Natt) very patient husband. On a recent day, the stuffed dog was dressed in full Judy Garland, Wizard of Oz garb, complete with ruby slippers, and set against a wrought iron railing on the open second floor, which made it almost the first thing a visitor to her home sees.

Needless to say, the dog is a precursor of things to come.

Facing page: Equal parts toy store and colorful nook, Natt's kitchen displays a lighthearted style that "makes me happy."

The sitting area/living room on the first floor mixes and matches several bright colors along with fanciful decorative objects that have caught Natt's eye.

Life As Art

The metamorphosis of Natt's home from pretty-but-plain to bold-and-bright mimics the life cycle of the butterflies she raises from caterpillars on a side table in her dining room. (She is an adamant butterfly lover, and her garden has been constructed completely of plants either designed to feed or nurture the butterflies that flit through the area constantly.) She talks about a day several years ago, shortly after nursing both parents through long final illnesses, when she decided she needed to make a change. The way she describes it, before that her style was all Victorian charm, with chintz and wallpaper, flowers and soft colors. She wanted something different, a new project to help with her grieving process. She called her computer programmer husband at his job, announced that she intended to sell most of their furniture and decorative objects, and start over again. The ever-patient Mike agreed.

The way Natt tells the story, laughing heartily at the memory, almost everything went except for a

This small bedroom was originally painted in quiet colors (see inset). Natt spiced up the palette, and added shelves to display her treasures.

dining room table and a few other pieces of furniture. So did the wallpaper—and in fact, so did the house where the wallpaper was. Confessing that she and her family "love to move," Natt, Mike, and daughters Anna and Rebecca began looking for a different house. They found a relatively new home (built in 1977) in a spacious, tree-laden suburb. The house was decorated in a quiet, reserved style, which Natt said she initially found welcoming and restful.

For a short time.

After that, the white walls, white carpet, white everything, seemed to demand something more from her, Natt says. A little paint here, a few found objects there, and soon the

house began to serve as a giant canvas for an ongoing art project. The open floor plan of the home allows a view of each room from the other, with a raised second floor living room.

"I'm not afraid of color," Natt says. "Almost all of my friends have houses with normal beige walls. They love my house, but it's something they would never do themselves. They're all kind of reserved and well behaved," she adds with a chuckle.

You get a sense, talking with Natt, that laughter is an important part of this home. When her parents passed away, Natt says she wanted to celebrate how precious life really is.

"I wanted my home to reflect my joy in living," Natt says of her very personal style. "I guess it was as if after all of the grieving and death and crying, I just wanted something that made me happy."

Polka dots fill the house, particularly on the curtains Natt sewed herself. Never one to be afraid of mixing and matching, Natt has painted adjoining walls in her dining room in wildly different styles and colors—one wall has large green stripes, another has pale yellow-orange diamonds in a harlequin pattern, and yet another is painted in a bright raspberry shade. Anchoring the dining room, and providing a transition from the first floor up to the second floor living room, is an enormous mural that Natt painted herself, using the image from the end of a pear crate as visual inspiration. She studied the image on the crate, and then re-created it on her wall using acrylic paints, completing the project in a few days.

Using the Canvas

From Natt's standpoint, the open floor plan of her home gives her a large number of "spaces" with which to work, including many walls that are separated from each other with corners or architectural details such as steps. Each flat area became a unique space that could be decorated with objects or color, and remain part of the whole while still standing on its own.

A large white wall seemed to deserve its own special touch: Natt added a large wall mural inspired by the image on a wooden pear crate.

Consider the kitchen. This modestly sized room is narrow, stretching along one side of the main floor. When Natt bought the house, an island was centered lengthwise in the center of the kitchen, providing usable workspace, but dividing the walkways into two narrow strips on either side. Natt studied the problem for a while before deciding that there had to be a better way to use her space. She found a crowbar and proceeded to do a little home remodeling, brute-force style. (Luckily, she discovered that the island was simply attached to the tile floor with an adhesive.) She managed to pry the island up, and reposition it sideways against the main wall that runs through the kitchen. To spice up its

Collections of items fill the house. **Above:** *A vaguely Wizard of Oz-inspired collection sits on a shelf over the dining room table.* **At right:** *A casual grouping of dolls, puppets, and toys sits near the entryway.*

rather humdrum appearance, she covered the top of the island with a bright red washable oil cloth, and then added bead board (available at any home improvement center) to the ends of the island to give it a more homey appearance. By repositioning the island, she maintained her work space, but added visual appeal to the room as well.

She dislikes the wall that runs lengthwise through the center of the first floor, separating the dining room from the kitchen, but has made her peace with it, at least temporarily. She would like to remove the wall, but until then, she has added two glass blocks to the space to the upper left of the island, letting light come through the area while still maintaining the wall's structural integrity. Colored paper lanterns, more often seen at a patio party, decorate the kitchen with pinks, yellows, and purples. Old postcards, toys, plastic fruit, and even a rubber chicken (don't ask) all add to the sense of lighthearted merriment in what is, in most homes, purely a functional room.

Before

Natt redecorated a bathroom with bright polka dot wallpaper, a mirror with a handpainted edge, and bits of whimsy such as an antique hat and old seed packets.

Natt made this checkered tile floor cloth under her dining room table using single 12-inch square tiles from a home improvement store. This inspired our project on page 74.

One key to Natt's personal collections hinges on an easy tip that anyone can use to transform a space into a showcase for objects that have meaning to their owner. Natt has added inexpensive shelves to many rooms in her house to hold like-minded items. In one bedroom, which was attractive but rather unremarkable when she bought the house, she added a continuous line of shelves slightly below the ceiling of the room. Each shelf also has pegs below it which gave her an opportunity to fill the room with a collection of dolls, old Raggedy Ann memorabilia, and other decorative items such as straw hats. By painting the room a dark burgundy yet leaving the shelving white, Natt draws attention to the collections without overpowering the small room.

Few questions stump the gregarious Natt, but the big one, "why?", does give her some pause. Why this style? Why these items?

"I want to live in a house that's original," she says after a moment. "I want to be able to use any color in any room," and not have to worry about the fact that "I can't use this here—there's no green in this room."

And besides, she adds with a grin, not many conventional decorating themes give a person the freedom to hang stuffed wooden poodles from the ceiling.

The other changes Natt has made in her space are less physical, but perhaps more emotional.

Here and there throughout the house are little vignettes, grouped items that tell a story, or that work together based on some theme. There is the vaguely Wizard of Oz -inspired collection that is gathered on a shelf over the dining area. An old placemat that depicts the Wizard of Oz movie, a large red doll house, alarm clocks, an old trophy that looks a bit like an Oscar and a small tree bedecked with white lights all cluster together in that spot, making an impact larger than the sum of the items.

On the entryway wall, Natt has collected another group of unique objects. One particularly charming decoration is a, well, sort of a "pig puppet."

Natt laughs when a visitor asks about the story behind that one. It seems her 4-year-old nephew created a face from a piece of an old cardboard egg carton while playing with some art materials. Natt liked the look of the piece, and decided to add legs, hair, and some other details to transform the face into a small doll-like decoration. The other items seemed to fit with the unusual decoration and eventually a small collection had gathered in that spot.

Natt decided the only thing this wooden poodle needed to achieve perfection was an outfit and a toy tiara.

Vintage Checkerboard Table

With a simple paint technique, an old dressing table finds new life as a piece of faux history.

Old furniture has a way of slipping from a useful object to just another piece of clutter in the basement or garage. That's unfortunate, because a well-made table or other piece can have multiple lives, refreshed from time to time with a bit of creativity and an eye toward the future, rather than the past.

That's what happened to this elegant old table, which was set at the curb at a neighborhood garage sale. Though a bit worse for wear, with numerous scuffs and bumps, the table still had a gentle charm all its own, with thin but sturdy legs and solid construction.

Rather than disguise the table's bumps and bruises, we decided to enhance them, and create an old-fashioned checkerboard game table that looks as if countless hands have slid checkers across it during evening games for years.

The whole project takes less than a weekend, including drying time. To make your own "faux-old" game table....

To Make a Checkerboard Table You Will Need:

- ◆ An old table
- ◆ Primer
- ◆ Painter's tape
- ◆ Paint for table
- ◆ Various acrylic paints for board
- ◆ Clear paint glaze
- ◆ Dark antiquing glaze
- ◆ Brush
- ◆ Artist brush

- ◆ Black paint pen
- ◆ Paint pan
- ◆ Tape measure
- ◆ Soft cloth
- ◆ T-square or other straightedge
- ◆ Sandpaper or electric palm sander
- ◆ 24 1-inch-diameter wood lozenges (available at craft stores)

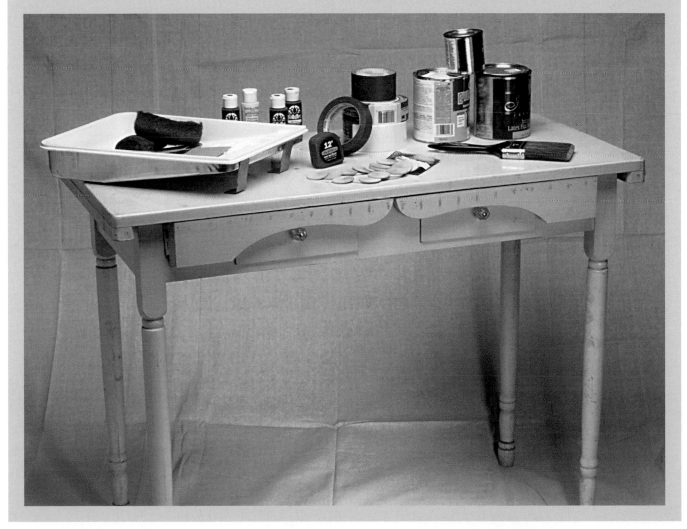

1 To provide a clean working surface, wash the table with soap and water to remove any dirt or grease and let dry. Remove any drawers and hardware, if necessary. Then, using a good quality paint primer (particularly if the old paint on the furniture is oil-based), paint the entire surface of the table.

2 A standard-size checkerboard contains 64 alternating dark and light squares, with 32 squares on each side of a center line. There are eight stacked rows of eight squares each on a board.

We decided to make each square 2 inches by 2 inches, for a total width and height of 16 inches by 16 inches. The "checkers" we selected are 1-inch wood lozenges, available at any craft store.

We used a ruler to mark off the square on the tabletop and lightly penciled in our lines. We used narrow painter's tape to create a ½-inch border outside our square.

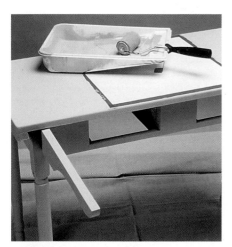

4 To simplify painting, we used wide painter's tape to mark off our grid. This gives nice clean lines to the squares, but it involves a four-step process, where you paint half the red squares, then half black, then the remaining red, and the remaining black. If you prefer, you can paint the squares freehand and skip the masking process.)

Create an alternating grid by placing three strips of 2-inch painter's tape lengthwise down first. (Note: Some 2-inch painter's tape is actually slightly narrower than that. If necessary, use a second strip of tape applied over the first to make your grid exactly 2 inches wide.)

3 Paint the rest of the table, leaving the board pattern unpainted. We used a faded green shade.

Press three strips perpendicular to these on top, to leave open 16 squares. (You'll repeat this step again later by removing the top three pieces of tape and adding three additional pieces over the dried painted areas to create spaces for 12 black squares.)

5 Using a water-based acrylic paint, paint each of the exposed squares red and let dry thoroughly. (Because we wanted a muted, old-fashioned color palette, we chose to paint our "red" squares in a soft plum color.) Once the squares have dried thoroughly— about 15 minutes—remove the top layer of tape, shift the position of the painter's tape, and create the remaining red squares. Using the same paint, paint 12 wood lozenges red, and 12 black. These will be your checkers.

6 Repeat steps 4 and 5 to complete painting the black squares.

7 We added a 1-inch border outside our painted checkerboard in a dark green. Use additional painter's tape to keep lines clean.

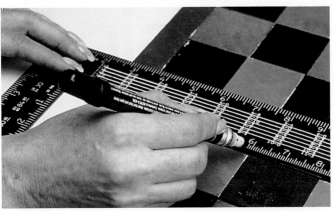

8 Remove all tape once the board and border have dried. Use a black paint pen and a straightedge to trace around the edges of all squares to create a clean border.

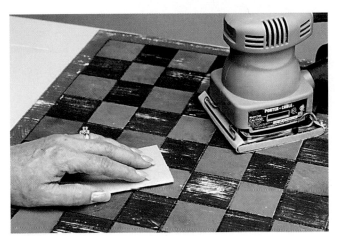

9 To give the table a distressed, "antique" appearance, use fine-grained sandpaper to lightly scuff the paint, or, if you wish, use a handheld palm sander to lightly distress the paint. Sand the table lightly in one direction only, and then go back and scuff individual squares to remove a small amount of paint and give the illusion of wear.

10 To further the illusion of age, we used an antiquing technique on the whole table to create a warm patina. We mixed a small amount of yellow acrylic paint with a dark antiquing glaze, available at any craft store. Thin the mixture with clear glaze until it is fairly liquid. You will need about ¼ cup of paint mix to cover a small table.

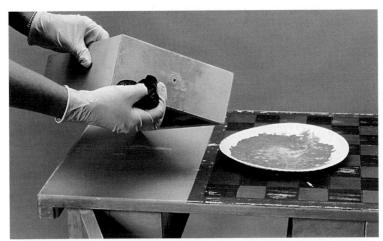

11 Dip a soft cloth or old cotton rag into the paint/glaze mix and gently wipe it across the table, taking care to work quickly and smoothly across the entire table until it has achieved a warm patina. Let dry thoroughly.

12 To protect your tabletop from future wear, you may wish to paint it with a clear coat of shellac or varnish after you have finished.

Classic Tile Floor Cloth

This technique lets you transform inexpensive floor tiles into a durable, washable floor covering that is loaded with style.

There's something immensely cozy about a checkered-tile floor covering. Whether the tiles are black and white, green and gray, or some other combo, this old-fashioned look is welcoming and wonderful.

We spotted a floor covering like this one in Cheryl Natt's house—see page 69—and it inspired this project. We used inexpensive individual vinyl floor tiles, each 12-by-12 inches, to create our own 5-by-7-foot floor cloth in a black-and-gray check pattern. You'll find these tiles available at any local home improvement store. Ours came from Home Depot, which offers a wide range of colors that will help you create your own custom look.

The floor cloth we completed is a relatively large one, but this technique can be sized to your own space or desires. For instance, you could create a long "runner" for a hallway that is three tiles wide and as long as necessary. Or you can make this a 3-by-5-foot floor cloth by following the instructions below and simply changing the number of tiles you use.

A couple of notes before starting: This is a project that requires a large, flat, well-ventilated work space, and it's easiest to complete if you have a helper. (It's also best to make this floor covering in an area where you can leave the piece undisturbed for a day or so while the adhesives set.)

Finally, all the steps for this project apply to the BACK of what will be your finished floor cloth. After you complete the final step, you will turn the piece over for use, so remember to work from the back of your tiles as you proceed.

To Make a Tile Floor Cloth You Will Need:

- ◆ Graph paper
- ◆ Marking pen
- ◆ Individual floor tiles (for our 5-by-7 floor cloth, we used 18 black and 17 gray tiles)
- ◆ Duct tape
- ◆ Utility knife
- ◆ Two plastic drop cloths
- ◆ Contact cement
- ◆ Two 12-inch short-nap rollers and trays
- ◆ Scissors
- ◆ 9-by-12-foot rubber-backed canvas drop cloth*

For the edging:
- ◆ Four black rubber transition strips 8 feet long and 1½ inches wide**
- ◆ Miter saw
- ◆ Utility knife
- ◆ Contact cement
- ◆ Small sponge applicator
- ◆ Several wood scraps as long and wide as your rug
- ◆ Clamps

*These professional quality drop cloths are used by painters, and should be available anywhere painting supplies are sold.

** Transition strips will be sold wherever individual floor tiles are sold. These strips are designed to provide a "transition" from a vinyl tile floor into another room or area. These strips have a deep groove in them that will accept the edge of the vinyl flooring.

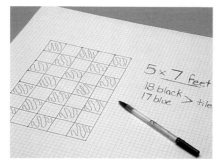

1 Plan the finished floor cloth by drawing a plan to scale to determine the number of tiles required, and to use as your guide when assembling the piece.

2 This floor cloth is assembled by first creating seven individual rows of tiles, each five tiles wide. Our tiles are secured together from the back using duct tape, alternating the colors to correspond with the design layout.

Spread a plastic drop cloth over your work area. Place your first tile on a flat surface. Butt the second contrasting tile to the first. (To ensure that the tiles you are taping together stay flush, place a third loose tile against the bottom edge to use to square up the first two.) Run a strip of duct tape down the seam between the first two tiles, cutting it to length with a utility knife. Leave about ¼ inch of space at the top and bottom of the tile seam uncovered by tape, since this will help you ensure that all four corners are lined up when attaching the 5-foot lengths together in the next step.

SPECIAL TIP

To create a checked pattern that alternates the length of the piece, you need an odd number of tiles in each row. If you're making a single-color runner, you can use as few as two tiles per row.

3 Begin attaching the 5-foot tile strips together with duct tape. Ensure that all seams and corners are lined up and edges are flush. Tape tiles together in an "X" pattern where the corners of the four tiles line up. Continue this process with the remaining 5-foot strips.

4 Run a strip of duct tape across the 5-foot lengths of tile to further reinforce the seam.

5 To reinforce the now-completed floor cloth, we attached the entire piece to a backing made from a rubberized drop cloth.

To do this, first cut the 9-by-12-foot rubber-backed drop cloth in half lengthwise. You now have two pieces of cloth that measure about 9-by-6 feet. Cut one cloth in half again so that you have two pieces that measure about 6-by-4½ feet. (Working with smaller pieces makes it easier to apply to the back of the tiles.)

Place the two smaller canvas drop cloth pieces on your plastic drop cloth, rubber-side down.

6 Make sure your work space is well ventilated before beginning this next step, since the fumes from contact cement can be strong. Follow manufacturer's instructions on the particular product you are using.

Apply contact cement to the back of your tiles. Move to the outside edge of your rubber-backed drop cloths. Starting about 6 inches in from the edge, apply contact cement to the cloth. (The cloth is larger than necessary and leaving the outside 6 inches uncemented will give you a clean edge to grasp when applying the cloth to the back of the tile.) We found that using a roller to apply the contact cement was quicker and easier than working with a brush. When applying the cement to the drop cloth, roll in one direction only.

7 (Have a friend help with this step.) The contact cement will look glossy and be tacky to the touch after 15 to 20 minutes (drying times may vary). Have one person hold the clean edge of one drop cloth up and away from the tile. The second person should smooth the fabric onto the tile surface, working from an edge. Use a clean 12-inch paint roller to press the cloth onto the tile. Add the second piece of drop cloth, butting seams together. Trim off excess material. Any loose spots may be further secured with a drop or two of contact adhesive.

8 To finish the edges of the floor cloth, we added black rubber transition strips to each side, cutting the corners at a 45-degree angle.

With the tile face-side down, pre-fit all of the edging pieces around the entire rug, cutting the corners at a 45-degree angle with a miter saw. We found it easier to start with our longer 7-foot strips and then to measure and cut the 5-foot pieces. Make sure the fit is snug around the entire rug. Once the strips fit well, mark them "top" and "bottom," "side right" and "side left". Remember: Since you are working with the rug face-side down, the right side becomes the left and vice versa.

9 Measure the lip of the edging strip. (Ours measured 1 inch.) Draw a 1 inch line around the outside portion of the entire floor cloth.

Place scrap pieces of wood under the edge of the tile to lift it slightly off of your plastic drop cloth surface. Apply contact cement with a small sponge applicator around the floor cloth, being careful to stay inside the 1-inch line. Apply the contact cement to the edge of the tile, as well.

10 Apply contact cement with a small sponge applicator to the lip of the rubber edging. In order for the edging strip to properly adhere to the tile, make sure the contact cement is also applied to the inside groove of the edging strip. Any excess contact cement can be removed with mineral spirits.

NOTE

Although the rubberized drop cloth will keep the tile floor cloth from slipping on most floors, it's a good idea to purchase and use a rug floor liner under the tile cloth to make sure it does not mar any floor surfaces.

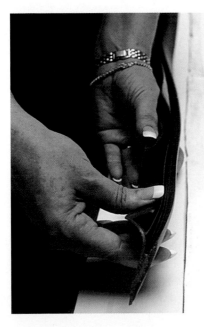

11 You'll need a friend's help for this step, as well.

Wait 15 to 20 minutes, until the contact cement appears glossy and is tacky to the touch (drying times may vary). Have a friend hold the length of the strip away from the tile edge. The second person will begin attaching the edging strip to the tile, starting at the corner. The person attaching the edging should pull the lip of the strip towards him or her, tilting the strip down so that the groove of the strip comes in contact with the edge of the tile first. Follow by pressing the lip of the edging strip against the rug. Be patient and work slowly to make sure the strips fit snugly.

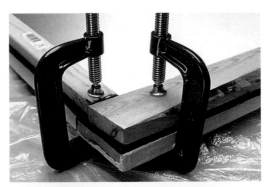

12 After you have attached all the edging, place scraps of lumber over the strip and weight or clamp in place. Let the contact cement set for at least 4 to 6 hours to ensure that the edging properly adheres to the tile. After the cement has dried completely, turn the rug over. (The tiles may bend as you flip the rug, but the tape and backing will keep all the tiles firmly in place.)

Adorable Armoire

Transform a ho-hum storage cabinet into an elegant armoire for less than $175.

When it comes to flexible, inexpensive storage, assemble-them-yourself cabinets work admirably. Often made of a substance called "melamine," which is a coated, pressed wood product, these cabinets provide extra storage space for minimal money. Cabinets such as these are sold in a wide variety of home and discount stores for around $100, depending on size.

Unfortunately, while these cabinets excel at utility, they sometimes leave a bit to be desired, decor-wise. Boxy and built for function rather than beauty, these storage systems are workhorses—but they may seem more suited to the garage than the guest room.

However, in a weekend or less, and with very little expense, you can transform a simple utility storage system into an elegant armoire. Better yet, once you've dressed up the frame with decorative molding and some picture frames, you have a versatile piece that can serve as colorful storage for a child's room, or can be dressed up in a more adult style to give you both flash and function.

This cabinet treatment is a flexible one, in that the finished "shell" can be painted or embellished to match any decor. We decorated this same cabinet two ways, using the same basic treatment and changing only the painting style. You can add extra color and texture using pressed wood cutouts, stencils, and a wide variety of other craft items. Since the frame remains the same, this armoire can also change with your style. If you tire of a certain look, you can paint and decorate this same piece over and over again to match any mood.

To Create This Armoire You Will Need:

- ◆ Heavy-duty melamine wardrobe cabinet (Ours came from Home Depot and measures 30 inches wide by 24 inches deep and is 70 inches tall)
- ◆ Six 11-by-14-inch picture frames
- ◆ Needle-nosed pliers
- ◆ Sawhorses or workbench with clamps
- ◆ Measuring tape
- ◆ Pencil
- ◆ Straightedge or T-square
- ◆ Safety goggles
- ◆ Drill, drill bits and countersink bits
- ◆ 1¼-inch drywall screws
- ◆ Four 8-foot pieces of ½-inch pine cove molding
- ◆ 1-inch finishing nails
- ◆ One 8-foot piece large crown molding*
- ◆ One 8-foot piece of 2-by-2 wood
- ◆ 2½-inch drywall screws
- ◆ Wood glue
- ◆ 1½-inch finishing nails
- ◆ White wood filler
- ◆ Primer designed for laminate finishes
- ◆ Screwdriver
- ◆ Fine sandpaper
- ◆ Miter box*

*Crown molding is decorative wood most often used around the ceilings in homes, and it comes in several sizes and must be cut at an angle to fit the cabinet. Review Step 16 before purchasing your molding.

Before

1 Assemble the cabinet, following manufacturer's directions. Our cabinet was originally intended as a wardrobe, and came with a fixed rigid upper shelf, and an optional clothes pole inside. (Look for a cabinet that offers good quality, heavy-duty door hinges.) Although we assembled the complete cabinet to show you how it looks, you will save time by not securing the doors to the frame until you have finished the project.

2 For this project, we used six 11-by-14-inch lightweight picture frames. To prepare the frames, remove the glass and cardboard backing and discard. Using a needle-nosed plier, remove any metal tabs designed to secure the glass and frame back in place.

3 Place the doors from the cabinet hinge-side down across a pair of sawhorses, or on a similar work surface. Measure each door. Our doors were each about 15 inches wide by 70 inches tall. Measure the empty picture frames, from side to side, and top to bottom. Our 11-by-14-inch picture frames were each 13 inches wide and 16 inches tall, and we used these measurements to space the frames equally on each door.

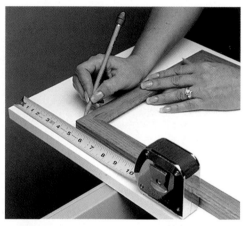

4 Place three frames on the front of one door, and use a pencil to draw along the outside and inside of each frame.

5 After tracing the frames, remove them and check your measurements. Use a straightedge or T-square to ensure that your lines are straight and square with the front of the door.

6 Repeat this step with the other door, again checking to ensure that frames line up on both doors.

7 Starting from the front of each door, carefully pre-drill through the center portion of each side of your "penciled" frame. You will be attaching the frames to the doors at these spots. Drill two holes on each side of each penciled frame, and two at both the top and bottom, making eight holes in each.

8 Turn the door over, and from the back, use a countersink bit to drill halfway through the door at the site of each pre-drilling mark. (Countersinking will hide the heads of the screws after you attach the frames.)

9 Flip each door right-side up, and use clamps to secure frames over the marks where each will be attached.

10 This step is easier if you have a helper. Set one door on its side on the sawhorses, having a friend hold the door securely. Working from the back of the door, use drywall screws to attach each frame to the door. We used 1¼-inch drywall screws because the door was ¾ inch thick, and the frame was also ¾ inch thick.

11 To conceal any gaps between the inside of our frames and the door, and for further decorative appeal, we added ½-inch pine cove molding inside each frame, creating a "frame within a frame." Use a miter saw to cut the molding to fit inside each frame, with 45-degree angles at each corner.

12 Attach the cove molding inside each frame with 1-inch finishing nails. Once you have attached the molding, set the doors aside for the moment.

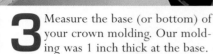

13 Measure the base (or bottom) of your crown molding. Our molding was 1 inch thick at the base.

14 Because our storage system had a flat top, we needed to create a base on the top of our armoire to which we could attach our crown molding. We did this by cutting three pieces of 2-by-2 wood to fit across the top and along each side of the top of our cabinet. Each piece of wood was set in from the outside edge of the top of the armoire 1 inch to allow the crown molding to sit flush against the edge of the cabinet.

15 Attach the 2-by-2 base to the top of the cabinet using 2½-inch drywall screws, following the pre-drilling directions used for the frames.

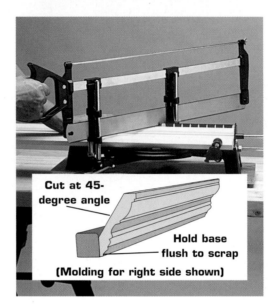

Cut at 45-degree angle

Hold base flush to scrap

(Molding for right side shown)

16 This cabinet uses three pieces of crown molding at the top of the cabinet. Cutting angles on crown molding can be confusing. If you have access to a power compound miter saw, this is a simpler process, and cuts should be made following the saw manufacturer's directions. These cuts can be made using a hand-powered miter saw, however. To cut the angle, butt the base of the crown molding against a piece of scrap wood as if it were already mounted on the cabinet, letting the front edge extend beyond the scrap wood. Make a 45-degree outside angle cut (see illustration) through the molding. Practice cuts with scrap wood before cutting the molding. If you are unsure of how to cut the molding, some lumberyards may be willing to cut it for you for a small fee.

17 Start with a side piece of the cut crown molding. Spread wood glue along the bottom and lower inch of the molding, and press it in place against your 2-by-2 base. Use 1½-inch finishing nails to secure the molding to the 2-by-2 support. Repeat with molding for the other side, and attach the front piece last.

18 Use wood filler, following label directions, to hide any small cracks where crown molding meets, and along the edge of the cabinet. Let dry.

19 After attaching all of your decorative wood, prime the entire cabinet using a good quality paint primer designed to be used over laminates. Let dry thoroughly, and then reattach the doors of the cabinet. Note: To ensure that any large upright cabinet doesn't tip, particularly if the cabinet is used in a child's room, you should secure the cabinet against a wall, following any manufacturer's instructions, if available. If you are remaking an old cabinet, or have misplaced the manufacturer's instructions, it is important to make sure the cabinet is securely bolted through the back cabinet wall into a stud as a safety precaution.

20 Once our primed cabinet had dried completely, we used stencils and wood cutouts in the shape of stars to create a "Star Light, Star Bright" theme for a child's room. Each frame was painted in a contrasting color, and the child's rhyme was drawn inside the frames using colored paint pens. We painted a sun in one corner, and hot-glued painted wooden stars both inside the frames, and on the frame edges themselves. You can add any embellishments to the finished cabinet you wish. See the photo at right for a different paint treatment of this same cabinet.

Here's the same cabinet, painted in a soft and feminine fashion. Use flower stencils and light colors.

New Life for an Old Sofa

These easy, relaxed slipcovers—and an optional repair for worn sofa arms—can freshen up a tired piece of furniture.

Before

Sofas and armchairs may be the most used—and abused—pieces of furniture in our houses.

We launch ourselves into them after a long day at work. The dog sneaks up on them while our backs are turned. The kids rub sticky hands across the material after we've told them for the one-millionth time to stop eating in the living room.

After all that, it's not surprising that these beloved pieces can look a little shopworn before their useful life is through.

That was the case with this small sofa and a matching chair. The original fabric—once an attractive off-white—had become a decidedly unattractive very off-white. However, the basic construction of the piece remained solid, although the hardwood frame underneath the arms could be felt in places.

Cleaning the pieces no longer produced satisfactory results, and because the pieces were slightly off-size, commercially available slipcovers never fit well—and were expensive, to boot. Besides that, conventional slipcovers never stayed in place during normal use, tending to slip and slide all over the furniture.

That was the dilemma. Some homeowners might have made the decision to toss out the pieces, and buy new, but that seemed wasteful. Besides, the pieces were well loved, both for their comfort and their versatility.

We came up with a unique option that gave these pieces a new lease on life, and that cost less than $200 for repairing both. We created a loose, relaxed slipcover for both pieces out of a medium-weight upholstery fabric, and solved the "slipping" problem by re-covering the cushions themselves in the same fabric. Not only did this refresh the pieces, the covered cushions are practical and secure the slipcover underneath firmly in place.

If you can sew a seam, you can create the slipcovers shown here. In general, a single very large piece of material is placed over the piece, and then "tucked" in place. Re-covering the cushions takes a little more work and more advanced sewing skills. However, the good news is that you can have seat cushions professionally re-covered by an upholstery shop for a fraction of the cost of reupholstering an entire piece. Shops we spoke to suggested that cushions could be re-covered in a customer's own fabric for around $40 each. Compare that to the price of new furniture, and you'll consider this a bargain any day.

A few tips before we get started: Before deciding to slipcover your furniture, check the condition of the frame, cushions, and coils. The underlying furniture must be in solid condition. When selecting fabric for your slipcovers, choose 54-inch fabric if possible, and a fabric that has little or no repeat is easiest to work with. Placing newly upholstered cushions over a loose slipcover also gives you a chance to change the look of your sofa by changing the fabric on the seat cushion in the future. Keep that in mind when selecting your background fabric. If you have an active household, choose fabrics that are washable, such as polyester/cotton blends.

If you want an even more relaxed look, you can create these slipcovers from good-quality bed sheets, since sheets are extra wide, and will require fewer seams. Sheets are also very washable and may be less expensive.

Finally, if you like the idea of this project but don't trust your sewing skills or simply don't have the time for this project right now, purchase a loose slipcover, and then have your cushions professionally re-covered in a complementary fabric. Place the purchased slipcover on the sofa underneath the cushions, and tuck the excess material into the sides of the piece. Place the cushions over the slipcover, and voila! You have a brand-new look for little money.

After

To Make Your Own Slipcovers You Will Need:

- ◆ Measuring tape
- ◆ Several large, old sheets
- ◆ Painter's tape
- ◆ Decorative fabric*
- ◆ Safety pins
- ◆ Scissors, thread, straight pins
- ◆ Covered Button Kit**
- ◆ Decorative tassels**

* Follow instructions in Steps 1 and 2 before purchasing your decorative fabric to ensure your measurements are accurate. If you are going to repair the arms of your furniture as described on page 91, complete those steps before measuring for your slipcover.

**We added small tabs at the corners of our slipcovers to provide a more tailored look. We secured these tabs with decorative covered buttons, which requires buttonholes in the tabs. If your buttonhole skills are rusty, secure the tabs in place with safety pins and disguise the pin itself with a decorative tassel.

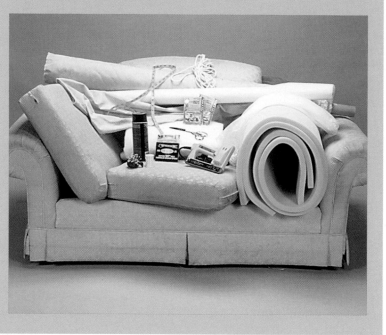

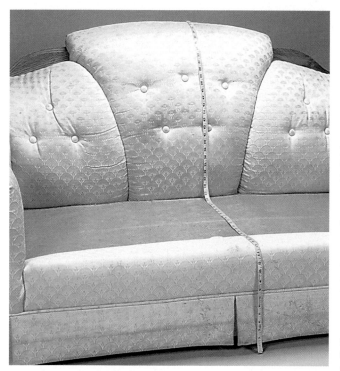

1 Remove the cushions from your chair or sofa and set aside. Use a cloth measuring tape or a long piece of string to measure the width (side to side) of your piece. Let the tape hang straight down from the arms to the floor. Add 10 inches to this number (for tucking) and record this measurement. Now measure the length of your sofa (front to back), add 10 inches (for tucking), and record this number.

As an example, our sofa (side to side) measured 132 inches, plus another 10 inches for tucking. That gave us a width of 142 inches. The sofa length (back to front) was 95 inches, plus 10 inches for tucking, for a total of 105 inches.

To calculate the number of yards of fabric you need for your slipcover, start with the measurements you recorded above.

Take your sofa width (side to side) and divide this by the width of your fabric. (Ours was 142 inches divided by 54 inches, which equaled 2.63 widths.) Round up to nearest whole number. We needed 3 widths of fabric.

Take the sofa length (front to back) and multiply that by the number of widths above, and then divide by 36 inches to find the number of yards required. (Our sofa measured 105 inches multiplied by 3, divided by 36, for a total of 8¾ yards.) Round up to the nearest whole number. We needed 9 yards of fabric for our slipcover.

To calculate the fabric needed for the seat cushions, measure the width and length of each cushion, plus its height. Our cushions were 24 inches by 24 inches, and were about 4 inches tall. These standard-sized cushions each needed about 1½ yards of fabric.

So, for our sofa, we needed 12 yards of fabric (9 yards for the slipcover, and 3 yards for the two seat cushions).

Note: It is always a good idea to purchase 1 to 2 yards of extra fabric, just in case! If you don't end up using it, store it for future use. You never know when a glass of red wine or grape soda will end up on one of your cushions.

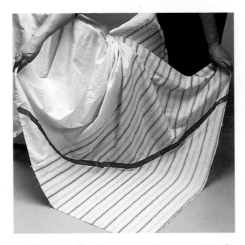

2 Before cutting your decorative fabric for the slipcover, experiment with this technique using old sheets. This gives you the opportunity to check the fit and the overall finished look of your loose slipcover and will let you adjust your pattern if necessary.

We used two large, old sheets sewn together and then cut into a single piece of fabric that was large enough to drape over our sofa.

3 These slipcovers are tucked tightly into the sides and edges of the furniture, under where the cushion will go. Extra fabric at the front of each arm, and in back, will be gathered together in a later step, so disregard the extra fabric here for the moment.

If you like the look of your slipcover as it stands, skip the rest of this step and move on to Step 4.

When we practiced tucking in our "sheet slipcover," we did not like the amount of extra fabric that puddled on the floor in each corner. We fixed this by marking the part of the fabric we wanted to trim away on the front and back in order to make a simple curved template to help us trim our decorative fabric later on.

Mark where the extra fabric falls on each corner of your slipcover with painter's tape. Place a sheet of paper over the taped marks on your sheet, and trace a rough template that matches the taped marks. Do this for each arm, and each side of the back of the slipcover, and mark on the template, "Front arm" or "Back corner." This will help later when positioning the template on your fabric.

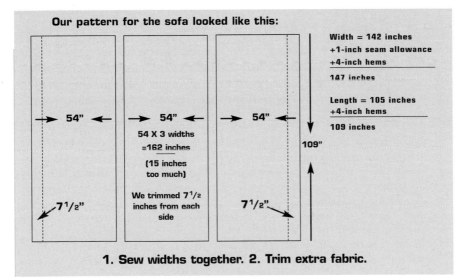

Our pattern for the sofa looked like this:

54" ← → 54" ← → 54"

54 X 3 widths
=162 inches

(15 inches
too much)

We trimmed 7½ inches from each side

7½" 7½"

Width = 142 inches
+1-inch seam allowance
+4-inch hems

147 inches

Length = 105 inches
+4-inch hems

109 inches

109"

1. Sew widths together. 2. Trim extra fabric.

4 The easiest way to measure and cut the fabric for your particular slipcover is to make a paper diagram that includes the measurements for your piece of furniture. Add allowances for seams and hems to your paper diagram to help you keep track of your measurements.

Our diagram looked like this: Our sofa width was 142 inches. We added 1 inch for seam allowances, plus 4 inches for a double-fold, 2-inch hem. That gave us a total of 147 inches.

Our sofa length was 105 inches, plus 4 inches for a double-fold, 2-inch hem, for a total of 109 inches.

Cut 3 widths of fabric 109 inches long. Sew widths together using ½-inch seam allowance. We now had a very large piece of fabric that measured 162 inches wide (3 widths of 54-inch fabric) by 109 inches long. Our fabric was 15 inches wider than we needed, so we cut 7½ inches from each side (to keep our seam lines straight on each side). That gave us a piece that was 147 inches wide by 109 inches long. Press seams open.

5 If you want to trim away extra fabric from the corners of your slipcover, as we did, use the drawing you made from the practice sheet slipcover. If you are happy with the look of the fabric on your piece, skip ahead to Step 6.

Pin templates in place on the front and back corners of your fabric. Trim away excess, following the pattern. Tip: If there is a slight variance in your templates for the front and back of the slipcover, use a fabric marker on the wrong side of the fabric to show which end is the front. This will help when you put the slipcover on the furniture.

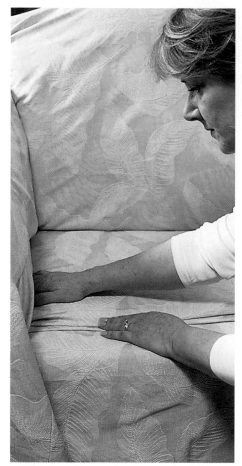

6 Press under 2 inches, twice, to the wrong side of the fabric to create a hem around the slipcover. Stitch in place using blind stitch or straight stitch.

Mark the center of your fabric at the front and back as well as the sides with a pin. Place slipcover over the furniture, lining up the center marks with the center of the front, back, and sides of your furniture. Use a couple of safety pins to keep the material roughly in place at these center points as you begin tucking.

Start tucking extra material into the sides and back of your sofa. Be patient, as this step takes some practice. Extra material under the seat cushion area can be folded back on itself, and then tucked in at the sides to keep the front and back edges of the slipcover even with the floor. Continue until you are pleased with the result.

7 This slipcover is designed to fall loosely on a sofa or chair. That means you will have extra fabric around each corner.

To give our slipcover a slightly more tailored look, we created small fabric tabs to gather this excess at each corner and secured the tabs in place with decorative covered buttons. (The buttons are optional, although they provide a nice touch. Covered button kits are available at any sewing or craft store. If you use the buttons, you will need to create buttonholes in the tabs. If you prefer not to do this, create the tabs as described below, and then fasten them to the fabric with safety pins as described later. You can disguise the piece of safety pin that will show on the front of the tab with purchased decorative tassels, if you wish.)

To create your own tabs, cut 8 pieces of fabric (2 for each corner) in any shape you like. (Ours were rough oblongs that measured about 3 by 7 inches.) With right sides together, using ½-inch seam allowance, sew two pieces together, leaving a small opening to turn the tab right-side out. Press and stitch opening closed.

Make a buttonhole about ½ inch in on each end. Cover buttons using a covered button kit (available at local fabric stores) and attach to the extra fabric using safety pins from the wrong side of material.

SPECIAL TIP

To make it easy to remove the buttons and tabs when laundering your slipcover, attach the buttons from the wrong side of the fabric using safety pins.

To Reupholster Box-Style Cushions You Will Need:

◆ Seam ripper/sharp, pointed small scissors
◆ Marker/masking tape
◆ 4-inch high-density foam*
◆ Upholstery batting*
◆ Zipper and glide*
◆ Welting/cording*
◆ Spray adhesive*
◆ Decorative fabric

*These items may or may not be necessary, depending on the style and condition of your cushions.

Note: You may find that some of the following steps do not correspond to your style of cushion, since cushions vary according to the piece of furniture for which they were made. We have included these steps to give you a general idea of how cushions are constructed. If you are a skilled sewer, you can adapt these steps to cover your particular cushion. If you prefer, take your cushions and material to a professional upholstery shop and have them repair the pieces for you.

If you plan to re-cover your own cushions, check the condition of the foam and zippers. Ours were in very good shape, with the foam still firm, and the zippers working well. The upholstery batting around the foam had lost its loft, which is very common. We decided to reuse all the foam and zippers on our existing cushions, but to add some new batting to give the cushions back their loft.

Most fabric stores carry foam, batting, welting, and zippers for upholstery. The type of foam most commonly used for seat cushions is 4-inch, high-density foam. If you need to replace the foam in your cushion, you can purchase this and cut it to size. This foam is not inexpensive, but it is still certainly less expensive than replacing the entire sofa. Zippers for upholstery are sold by the yard. Glides are sold separately.

Pay close attention to how your seat cushion was constructed when separating your existing seat cushion for a cutting pattern. If you are working with a piece of furniture that has more than one cushion, remove the cover from each cushion and use it as a guide while making your new covers.

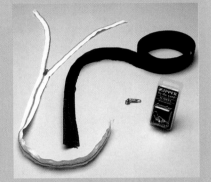

New zippers can be purchased by the yard at fabric stores.

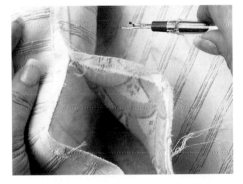

1 Remove the cover from a seat cushion to use as a pattern. Use a seam ripper or small scissors to undo all seams, separating all pieces. Pay close attention to how the seat cushion cover is constructed as you take it apart, because the pieces will go back together the same way. (It's not a bad idea to take notes as you pull apart the cover. Use a marker to write the name and position of each piece on the fabric itself, "Top of Seat," "Sides," "Zipper Back," and so on. If it is difficult to see the grain of the fabric, also mark the direction of the grain with arrows, "Front Top of Seat Cover," and so on.)

Close the zipper. Remove the zipper using the seam ripper. Place a piece of masking tape at the top and bottom of the zipper to keep it from coming apart during the process, since it can sometimes be difficult to put it back together.

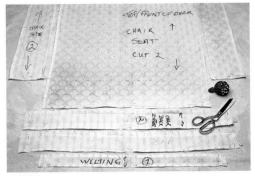

2 Press all seams flat. Place and pin all pattern pieces on decorative fabric. Cut all pattern pieces for each cushion. Tip: As some pattern pieces look very similar, it may be helpful to pin a small note to your new pattern pieces identifying what they are.

3 Start re-doing your cushion with the two-piece panels of the zipper section. Press under ½ inch to wrong side, lengthwise, on one side of each pattern piece. With right side facing up, pin side of zipper panel to zipper, lining up the turned edge with the center of the zipper. Install zipper foot on machine, aligning it to right side of needle. Sew zipper in place. Your seam should be approximately ¼ inch from turned edge. Repeat on opposite side of zipper. Zipper should be completely concealed. Tip: It is best to keep the zipper closed when attaching panels.

4 Install general-purpose sewing foot on machine. With right sides together, attach side panels to each end of the zipper panel, using ½-inch seam allowance. (Place a small piece of fabric over exposed zipper to avoid breaking your needle.) Backstitch over zipper area to secure. You should now have one continuous band of fabric.

5 To make welting, if your cushions require it, install zipper foot on machine, aligning it to right side of needle. Adjust stitch to a basting stitch length. Fold fabric over welting cord, aligning the cut edges of fabric. Stitch close to the cord, while continuing to fold the fabric over the cord as you sew.

6 Welting on seat cushions varies with furniture styles. Some are box-style cushions, with welting on top and bottom edge of seat. Our cushions had welting only in the center front of the cushion. Follow the same style previously used on your seat cushion. If you decide to skip this step, we suggest that you reinforce your seams with double stitching to secure.

7 Before pinning your side panel to the seat panels, mark the center of the front, back, and sides of the seat panels, as well as the side panel. (This can be done with pins or a fabric marker. If you use a marker, mark the wrong side of the fabric.)

To attach welting, pin welting to right side of seat cushion panel, lining up raw edge of welting to raw edge of seat cushion panel. Sew in place with zipper foot aligned to right side of needle. Stitch as close to cord as possible, removing pins as you sew. Repeat for additional welting.

With right sides together, pin the seat panel to side panel at markings. Continue pinning between each section until the entire seat panel has been pinned in place. Partially open zipper to allow access once the cover is sewn. Repeat the pinning process with the other seat panel. If your seat cushion has welting, install the zipper foot on machine, aligning it to the right side of the needle. Sew seat cushion to side panel, keeping the stitching close to welting. Repeat on opposite side. Clip any curved edges or corners to help fabric lay flat and eliminate puckering. Be careful not to clip through stitching. Turn cover right-side out and press.

8 (optional) If desired, cover seat cushion with a new layer of batting, securing it in place with spray adhesive. Only apply batting to areas where it was previously in place. Trim away excess batting, making it even with the foam.

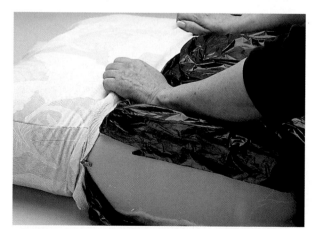

9 To make inserting the cushion into its new cover easier, slit the sides of a large garbage bag and wrap it around the cushion. The open end of the bag should be at the back of the cushion. Be sure the zipper is fully opened and insert the cushion into the cover. Adjust cover so that it is square with the cushion. Once cover is in place, remove the bag and close the zipper.

SPECIAL TIP

An upholstery shop will re-cover your cushions in a fabric of your choice for a small price. The slipcover itself is very simple to make.

To Restore Damaged Arms You Will Need:

◆ 1-inch high-density foam
◆ Lining fabric
◆ Upholstery batting
◆ Spray adhesive
◆ Electric staple gun and ½-inch staples
◆ Standard screwdriver

1 This is an optional project. If your chair or sofa arms are still in good shape, skip these steps. Our arms had lost most of their original "cushiness" since the foam inside had worn away, and the wood frame inside the pieces could be felt when you pushed on the arms of the piece.

Measure and cut a piece of 1-inch foam and the same amount of batting in a piece large enough to fit around the perimeter of the arm. (The foam doesn't need to cover the front or back of the arm.)

Cut a piece of lining fabric 8 inches longer and wider than the piece of foam and batting. (Covering foam with batting and fabric helps to protect the foam from breaking down.) Center foam and batting on lining, and secure using spray adhesive.

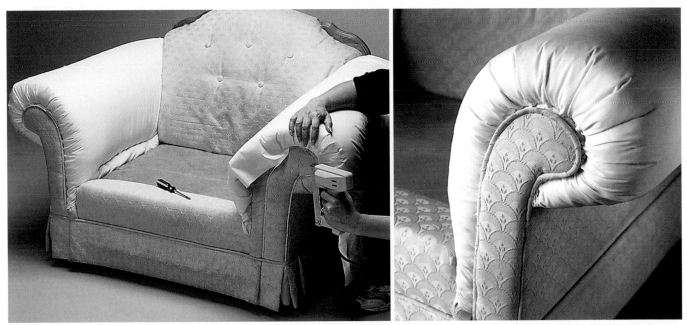

2 Center foam over the arm of the furniture. Using an electric staple gun and ½-inch staples, locate the hardwood frame of the furniture. Secure foam piece by placing a few staples through material into the frame at the front and back, as well as the inside and outside of the arm. Begin to staple foam in place, starting at the back of the arm, moving to the inside edge, and then to the outside edge.

Our sofa had a rigid fascia piece that decorated the front of each arm. We used a standard screwdriver to pull the lining fabric taut, while tucking it behind the fascia piece at the front of the furniture and then stapling the piece in place.

If your furniture does not have any fascia, create small pleats in the lining fabric and staple in place pulling the fabric taut as you staple. Trim away any excess fabric.

New Life for Old Linens

Classic old fabrics can be cleaned, repaired, and even dyed bold new hues.

When it comes to elegance, there's nothing quite like vintage linens.

The fine linen, cotton, and rayon textiles of the last century are of a quality not commonly found in today's linens, which is one of the reasons why they're still so widely sought after and used. Better yet, these beautiful tablecloths and other items were made to stand up to use, so it's a shame to leave them tucked away to languish in a drawer. Best of all, excellent dyes are available today that let you re-create these beautiful items with your own personal style. With a few simple steps, you can remake your linens in any color of the rainbow.

Chances are you have—or have access to—a treasure trove of family linens. Fine bedding, damask cloths, and embroidered finery were once essential elements of a woman's bridal trousseau. From exquisitely embroidered pillowcases to delicate quilting and crochet work, these items may have filled a hope chest of the last century.

Many of our mothers received wedding gifts of least one set of linens, such as a white damask tablecloth and napkins.

If you've missed out on your own family's heirloom fabrics, check out estate or tag sales. Get there early: Interest in collecting linens has grown steadily over the last 10 years and good specimens go fast.

Yard sales or thrift stores are another good source for vintage linens, but beware of hidden holes and stains. Antique stores carry linens that often are in excellent shape and which may already have been laundered and pressed for use.

Your best vintage finds don't always come with tags or labels, so how do you identify them? Textile experts talk about a fabric's hand—its feel, fluidity, and sheen. For example, the hand of linen is much finer than that of cotton. Rayon is shiny, and the degree of shine is influenced by what else is woven into the fabric. If you have access to old linens with their labels intact, compare them and familiarize yourself with their features. But if the linens are really old or are handmade, enlist the help of your mother, aunts, or grandmothers. Chances are they can tell you more about the fabric than a label would anyway!

Stains and Repair

Vintage linen is seldom in truly mint condition. Most collections have a rich past life and use may be evident in a stain or thin spot. Examine your linens thoroughly: Look for weak spots, stains, and the dreaded hole. (Don't despair, however. Small holes can be mended or—if it's a table-cloth—covered with a strategically placed vase of flowers or dinner plate.)

Old linens typically have old stains, but you'd be surprised at the results you can get with a little effort and some old-fashioned remedies (see "Lighten Those Linens" on page 94). Everything from pure cotton to fine linen and rayon can be returned to near-original glory. Use a long soak for stained fabrics—48 hours or more—in a laundry tub filled with hot water, a cup of Biz laundry detergent and a cup of 20 Mule Team Borax. This soak eliminates age discoloration and fold-lines present on long-stored linens. It also can reduce old food stains and brighten whites and colors—without chlorine bleach.

(By the way, never use bleach on linens—it speeds the deterioration of all cloth fibers. Instead, try spreading dampened linens on the grass in the sun. Squeeze lemon juice on stains and the sun will lighten them. For rust stains, use Whink, a product available in hardware stores or in some grocery store cleaning sections: Squeeze a few drops of this product directly on the rust spots and watch them evaporate right before your eyes!)

For new stains on old textiles, it's worth it to invest in a good stain-remover handbook. Different stains call for different treatments. Douse coffee stains with white vinegar, or dilute red wine stains with club soda followed by a paste of salt.

After soaking and treating your linens, launder them in gentle soap powder and rinse thoroughly. Line dry or try the delicate setting on your dryer.

Storing Linens

Whether your collection is large or small, it's important to know the keys to safekeeping valued linens. Always hand-wash vintage cotton, linen, and rayon. Use mild laundry soap and rinse thoroughly. Hang whites in the sun if you can. If you spill on a vintage cloth, treat the stain as soon as it's convenient to clear the table. Cool water is best, and if you're fast, you can prevent most staining simply by washing with laundry soap. Iron your linens only when you're ready to use them—ironed-in creases can hasten the breakdown of cloth fibers. I never starch my linens because if they sit for a while, the creasing itself can break down the fibers.

Fold your clean linens neatly but loosely, or roll them into cardboard tubes covered with cotton. Never set fine linens on bare wood shelves. Cover the shelves with shelf paper; acid-free is best and the paper stays effective for up to seven years.

Old Linens Reborn

The best thing about beautiful old fabrics is how much you can do with them, so free them from your drawers and boxes and find a place for them in your home. The decorative appeal of old linens depends on your taste, of course, but even if you prefer a contemporary look or are bored by all-occasion whites, you can deploy those floral print tablecloths as beautiful accent pillows or as a valence atop your kitchen window.

And even if your mother's linen tablecloths and napkins aren't in pristine condition, the elegant damask pattern will jump right off the fabric when you dye them an exuberant color. You can get fantastic results using a fiber-reactive dye called Procion MX, which is effective on all natural fibers such as cotton, rayon viscose, linen, and even wool and silk. Widely used in the textile industry since 1956, Procion dyes are colorfast and light-safe (resistant to fading). And you can dye linens virtually any color imaginable. Some merchants offer 100 color choices.

It is even possible to tinker with mixing these powdered dyes to create your own unique dye vat. Allow yourself 2½ hours to complete the job. Depending on the dye you select, follow manufacturer recommendations carefully. (You can pick up further instructions and dye materials at art supply stores.)

Imagine your table set with azure blue linen accented with lime green and royal purple napkins. No one will ever guess they were your great-aunt Sadie's. But do tell!

To Dye Linens You Will Need:

For linen, cotton, or rayon fabrics:
- A large plastic tub (large Rubbermaid totes work well)
- Rubber gloves
- Broomstick
- Plastic safety goggles
- Wet cloth for quick wipe-ups of spilled dye
- Linens
- Procion MX dye*
- Hot tap water
- Non-iodized salt
- Soda Ash Fixer*
- Synthrapol *

*Sources on page 95.

1 Pre-wash fabric using either a gentle laundry detergent, or the cleaner Synthrapol. (This product does an excellent job of cleaning linens prior to dyeing, and can be ordered from the Sources listed on page 95.)

Once you have pre-washed, dye your fabric while it's still wet from laundering. If you can't dye immediately, store clean, damp linens in plastic garbage bags for up to 24 hours.

2 When using any dye, put on rubber gloves and old clothes. Wear plastic safety goggles to protect your eyes from splashes. Work in a well-ventilated area where kids or pets won't intrude. Also, use the largest container you can find as a dyeing bucket, because you will need room to stir the dyes. Larger containers are also more difficult to accidentally tip over. For the specific type of dye used here (Procion MX), fill container with 3 gallons very hot tap water. These dyes use salt to develop the color; the amount varies with color chosen. (Manufacturer instructions include proportions with the color chart.) Add non-iodized salt and dissolve completely; add dye and dissolve completely.

LIGHTEN THOSE LINENS

To freshen stained or yellowed linens, try this presoak:
1 cup 20 Mule Team Borax
1 cup Biz
Dissolve in a laundry tub full of tepid-to-hot water; soak 48 hours or longer, depending on the degree of yellowing. Stir occasionally and rinse until water runs clear.

Another excellent presoak is the detergent Dreft, which I use for cleaning delicate cottons such as the fabric in batiste christening gowns or vintage baby clothes. Synthrapol (see Sources, page 95) is a good pre-wash and after-wash that helps remove invisible lubricants, dirt, and oil that can affect your dye results.

3 Most Procion dyes call for 1 tablespoon dye powder for 1 pound of fabric—approximately 3 to 6 square yards.) Dissolve powder completely.

4 Add damp fabric to bucket and, using broomstick, stir mix constantly for 20 minutes.

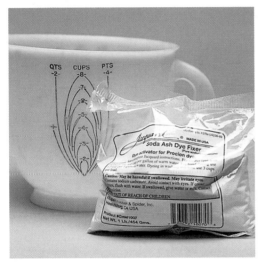

5 Once fabrics have been dyed, a separate product is often used to "set" the color—in this case, soda ash. (Instructions for fixatives come with the dye.)

In a separate container, dissolve fixer in 1 to 2 quarts HOT water. Add to tub. (Some Procion dye mixes call for adding a product called Calsolene Oil, a "wetting agent" to help colors take uniformly. I use the wetting agent for dyeing blue tones in particular because it's a difficult color to reproduce without variations in tone. At this point, depending on the color of dye you have selected, you will need to leave the material in the bath for an additional amount of time, again, with the time needed being noted on the dye selected.

6 Drain dye bath and rinse fabric thoroughly with cold water several times. Wash wet fabric in 3 gallons of hot water, to which you have added 1½ teaspoons of Synthrapol or other gentle liquid detergent. Rinse washed fabrics well and line dry or use delicate cycle of your dryer.

SOURCES FOR DYEING SUPPLIES

Most art supply stores stock dyeing essentials. The Procion dyes mentioned here are available from Dharma Trading Co. at www.dharmatrading.com or 800-542-5227. Dyes are sold in varying quantities, from 2 ounces to 110 pounds; prices vary by color and quantity (generally from $4 to $30). You can see colors and can order online, but call the toll-free number and get the catalog first to see color samples. The catalog is packed with textile craft supplies, including Soda Ash Fixer and the recommended laundry detergent, Synthrapol, for cleaning linens before and after dyeing. You can also order Calsolene Oil, a wetting agent that makes water "wetter" to promote more even dyeing.

Great Books

The Stain and Spot Remover Handbook, Jean Cooper, Storey Books, 1995. A practical manual for finding out what causes stains and what can remove them. Well organized for retrieving information in a hurry.

Vim & Vinegar, Melodie Moore, HarperCollins, 1997. Imaginative uses of vinegar, including environmentally healthy recipes for household cleaners. Includes tips for removing old stains from vintage fabrics.

Office Work

Unclutter and rearrange your home office and add some storage with style.

Simple two-drawer metal filing cabinets can be updated with new handles, paint, ball feet, and "upholstered" sides to give you storage and style.

Do you shut the door to your home office in embarrassment when company comes calling? Spend more time searching for critical papers than you do working? Do you even remember what the top of your desk looks like?

Home offices are changing from a luxury only a few can afford to a necessity for most of us. We need a place where we can settle in comfort when we bring extra work home, or just a quiet spot where we can retreat to pay bills.

No matter the initial intent for a home office, in many houses, this room becomes a catch-all for papers and other items, leading to confusion, clutter, and chaos. Wouldn't an inviting workspace that is as efficient as it is decorative be much better?

The first thing to do is to get organized. Once you've done that, you can add some personality to your home office with the decorative file cabinets we'll show you how to make, starting on the next page. But before we do that, let's get rid of the mess.

Getting Started

Start by getting three large cardboard boxes, and mark them "Toss," "Must Have," and "Need." Now it's time to start sorting.

The "Toss" box is self-explanatory. The "Need" box is for the things that you use only once in a while, say once or twice a month. The "Must Have" box is for items that you have actually used within the last week. Consider putting all of your "decorative" objects in the "Need" box for now, including photos, desk art, candles, and so on. You'll have a chance to add them back to your space later, but for now, you want to clean off every surface you can, including your walls, shelves, and desktop.

As soon as the "Toss" box is full, march it out to the garbage. Even if you're wracked with guilt because the gift you've always hated from your great aunt sits on top, be firm. If you have more to throw away, get a new box and start again.

Once the "Must Have" and "Need" boxes are full, slide them into another room, out of sight for now. If you need to, get more boxes, until everything in the room has been sorted.

Now that much of the room has been cleared out, it's time to look at the room itself. Start with the walls. Patterned walls can add confusion to an already busy room, so you may want to start with a great paint color. Chose a color that will calm and relax, such as green or blue.

Rearrange the Furniture

The next step is to arrange the furniture you already have, and consider which other items you may want to add.

Think about all the things that happen in your office. Do the kids study in front of the computer? Do you pursue handicrafts or other hobbies there? What else takes place in the office?

The goal here is to create a small nook where each specific activity can take place, with the supplies necessary for that function close at hand. Do you use your office to pay bills? A small desk in a corner, complete with pens, stamps, checkbook, and financial records, will contain that activity without lending clutter to the rest of the room.

One good option for many office spaces is to set your main worktable or desk in the middle of the room, placing a short end against the wall. This both allows access to the desk from all sides, and creates a natural room divider. The "Must Have" items from your box should all be within arm's reach of this desk. The "Need" items can be tucked farther away, perhaps in a cabinet on a far wall that can be closed to keep those items out of sight most of the time.

Use furniture and walls to define other areas in the room. A bookcase secured perpendicularly to a wall will create a cozy hideaway behind it. This is also a handy place to store large boxes or to tuck other larger items out of sight.

Next you'll need accessories to hold standard office supplies and aid in organization. There are many products available in home stores for this purpose, from paper clip holders to file cabinets. But take a look at what you have on hand first. Comb flea markets and resale shops for inexpensive alternatives. Look for function, since style and fashion can always be added. Here are some ideas to get you started.

Like antiques? An old four drawer cabinet not only looks good but will store an incredible amount of paper. Old fruit crates will hold a lot of items out of the way but still close at hand.

Don't be afraid of using cardboard boxes in different sizes to house all sorts of things. You can even spray paint good-sized boxes with lids and create labels for them by painting 1-inch by 2½-inch pieces of tag board and securing them to the box with photo corners.

Canister sets also work as well for storage in the home office. Thrift store finds can be painted and labeled in the same manner as the boxes. Or hang painted shipping labels from the lids' handles. Canning jars can add a sparkle to the storage area when filled with thumbtacks or paper clips, and the best part is that labels aren't

necessary. You can see what you have at a glance.

Bulletin boards keep important information in sight and clipboards can keep papers close at hand. Place a hook on the side of your worktable and hang the clipboard within reach, back side facing out. You can even paint the back of the clipboard with chalkboard paint to give yourself a place to jot down short notes.

When adding any storage unit to your office, think about dressing it up with fabric or paint to add color and warmth. Choose one accent color to use predominately throughout the room to unify it. Black is a good choice since no matter how color styles change, items in this color are always available. Other colors can be added in smaller amounts to provide excitement and fun.

The next step is to place supplies back into the room. The "Must Have" box comes in first. The "Need" box can be brought in next. If there still isn't room for everything in your office, it is time for more sorting. Place the items that you "might need someday" back in the box. Clearly label the contents and send the box to the attic or basement.

Finish by placing things that make you smile all around the room, and you'll soon find that your office door doesn't need to be shut when company comes to visit.

Chapter
three
Decorating

Put the fate of important decorating projects into your own capable hands. If you're armed with the right ideas and instructions, they're easy!

Decorative Throw Pillows

Colorful throw pillows pull a room together like nothing else.
By making your own, you can select fabrics and textures that
complement any decor.

Although decorative pillows are usually a relatively inexpensive accent piece, sometimes the choices available in stores just aren't what you want. If you make your own pillows, the choices of fabrics, trims, and textures can be exclusively yours. A little fabric and trim go a long way when creating these pillows, so splurge and make them from silk or tapestry fabric that would normally be too expensive for a large project.

Decorative pillows are a good way to refresh any room with just a little time and a little cash. If you use your imagination, you can also add whimsy to the pillows with decorative accents such as covered buttons or a piece of costume jewelry attached to one or two pillows with a silky tassel. The choice is up to you.

To Make Your Own Decorative Throw Pillows You Will Need:

For an 18-inch round pillow....
◆ Decorative coordinating fabrics
◆ Scissors, pins, thread
◆ Batting
◆ Decorative trims
◆ Welting
◆ Pillow forms
◆ Measuring tape
◆ Tape

Optional:
◆ Tassels
◆ Covered button kit
◆ Vintage jewelry

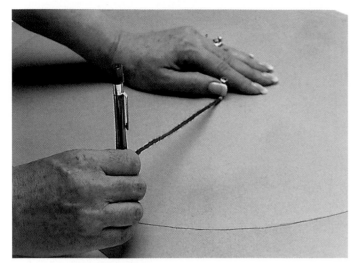

1 We made a round 18-inch decorative pillow with two contrasting fabrics, one on each side, centered around a covered button. To do this, you'll need a 19-inch round paper template. An easy way to make this template is to place a large piece of paper on top of a piece of cardboard or on a cutting mat. Tie a piece of string around a sharp pencil. Place a pin through the string, 9½ inches from the pencil. Place the pin in the center of your paper, and secure it by pushing the pin through the paper into the cardboard or cutting mat. Hold the pencil upright, pulling the string taut, and then draw your circle.

2 Using your paper template, cut two circles each from decorative fabric, lining, and batting. You now need to divide the lining fabric into eight equal, pie-shaped pieces.

To do this, fold the lining fabric in half, and use a fabric marker to trace along the fold line. Fold the lining fabric the opposite direction and mark on fold line again. (You now have four pie-shaped sections.) Fold and mark lining fabric twice more to create eight equal pie pieces.

SPECIAL TIP

We also created two 18-inch decorative pillows that were pieced together from complementary fabrics, and then embellished with a piece of trim that runs vertically through the center of the pillow. You'll find that decorative pillows look better with slightly rounded corners rather than square corners, since the pillow form seldom fills the fabric shell completely.

ADD A LITTLE FRINGE

We also made two 22-inch tapestry pillows detailed with fringe to complement our round pillow. If you want to add fringe to a pillow, tape the fringe ends in place away from the outside edge of the fabric to keep the tips from getting caught in your seam while you sew. (See example below.)

SPECIAL TIP

Depending on the style of decorative pillow you choose, your options for embellishing the piece are endless. Pillows can be enhanced with a covered button in the center of the pillow, with a piece of decorative costume jewelry, or with welting, fringe, or tassels.

3 Place decorative fabric on flat surface with wrong side of fabric facing up. Lay batting and marked lining fabric over wrong side and pin in place. Use several pins to keep fabric from shifting during sewing. Tip: Turn fabric over after pinning to be sure it hasn't puckered during the process. Set the stitch length on your sewing machine to a basting stitch. Starting at the center of the circle, sew toward outside edge, following fabric marker lines. Continue around circle until all markings have been basted.

4 To finish the pillow, you can either make your own decorative welting from contrasting fabric or use ready-made welting, fringe, or trims.

On right side of fabric, pin welting around outside edge of circle. It will be necessary to clip edge of welting approximately every 2 inches in order for it to lie flat. (Be careful not to cut through the stitched edge.)

Sew in place using zipper foot. Leave zipper foot on machine and sew back of pillow to front, leaving an opening to insert pillow form. Turn fabric right-side out, press and insert pillow form. Hand or machine stitch opening closed.

ADDING JEWELRY AND TASSEL ACCENTS

You can use a small safety pin to secure pieces of vintage jewelry or tassels to pillows for a decorative accent.

This is a great way to showcase unusual finds, or to use an earring that has lost its mate.

Unique Chic

This passionate collector has designed her home with taste, charm, and a style all her own.

When Jan Eisner sees something she really likes at a yard sale or at one of the thrift stores she haunts, chances are good that the item will find its way home with her. It doesn't really matter what the "treasure" is—a black vase, garden print, fruit plate, silver frame, Indian blanket, or crystal knob—if Eisner likes it, that piece has found a home. The only criterion for selection is that in some way known mostly to Eisner, it's unique.

Uniqueness is the principal feature and ultimate objective of Eisner's personal style, and of her home, as well. A close second is economy—or, more importantly, value. These two motivations drive just about everything she and her husband, Walter, have done in their charming old home.

That elastic philosophy of "attractive and affordable" provides dozens of opportunities for guiltless pleasure in collecting as well as in an ongoing house remodel that, out of necessity, has proceeded over the past dozen years under a strict budget.

Finding a Home

With its warmth, spaciousness, quirky collections, and one-of-a-kind features, Eisner's house is a work in progress. Purchased 12 years ago, the 118-year-old house was, of course, unique. But it was definitely a "fixer-upper."

Facing page: An old-fashioned parlor seems to encourage visitors to step back in time.

Vintage linens are one of Eisner's many passions.

Originally clapboard and bric-a-brac, the two-and-a-half story Victorian had been covered in stucco during an austere facelift in the 1920s. The formerly grand entry porch had been enclosed in aluminum combination windows; the entry itself had been replaced with a flimsy hollow-core door and glass-block sidelights. The roof leaked, the furnace was shot, and the windows rattled in the slightest breeze. A caved-in stable stood inaccessible behind a modern double garage. And what the Eisners thought must be hardwood flooring under the beige carpet turned out to be layers of linoleum over pine boards.

But the house overlooked a spacious park from a deep corner lot with mature trees. It had high ceilings, large rooms, great light, and touches of elegance—including two fireplaces with intricate mantels and an oak-paneled dining room. Some features were simply interesting, like an alcove in the stairwell. (The couple have since learned that the alcove probably was designed to accommodate religious statuary when the home was built in its Catholic neighborhood.)

The Eisners knew when they purchased their home that they weren't buying a trouble-free house. For them, however, the advantages trumped the problems. "We couldn't afford a grand new house, but old houses are grand even when they're not expensive," says Eisner. "There's a substance and uniqueness to old houses, a one-of-a-kindness. There are no rooms in this house that are square."

So taking the long view, the couple set about turning their old house into a home, finding time to fill it with objects they love, and with details they could afford, all acquired one at a time.

It is precisely those details that you first notice in this home. "Practically limitless" describes the variety of collections housed here. There's a wall covered with hand-painted Mexican wooden plates; the cherub prints on the bathroom wall; the 1920s-era posters; the sock monkeys; and the "critter collections" of bears, dogs, and fish. The only thing each of these collections have in common is Eisner's own pleasure at their existence. "I keep them because they make me smile," she says.

Because her collections are such a continuing source of pleasure, she never tires of rearranging them to keep them visually fresh. Three ceramic frogs that had become invisible on the mantel reappear on the bookshelves with a small spotlight. A half-dozen black vases that were on the corner of the buffet now march across the kitchen cabinets,

An old library cabinet was cut to fit Eisner's kitchen, and now holds a festival of collectible Fiestaware.

Determined Discovery

Contrary to her modest claims, Eisner's discoveries are no accidents: She invests hours hunting for treasures and scouring Web sites. "It's cheap entertainment," she says.

For example, she's a regular at a half-dozen carefully chosen thrift stores within a few miles of her urban neighborhood. On weekends, she often hits an estate sale or two, where she's found elegant display cases for her booths and nearly all the furniture in her house. Usually, she shops early and buys late, taking advantage of late-sale markdowns.

Vacations are not-to-be-overlooked opportunities for uncovering great deals. During one recent trip through a rural midwestern town, Eisner and husband Walter stopped at a junk shop and discovered a cabinet so perfect they remodeled their entire kitchen around it.

The cabinet—a glass-enclosed top over pine cupboards and drawers—is 9 feet long and nearly 8 feet tall. But the 9-foot, 2-inch kitchen ceiling was only 8 feet, 6 inches high in the middle of the wall, where the cabinet was to go, because of a foundation collapse in the 1950s. The couple resolved the problem by having the ceiling lowered to the level of its minimum height, and then they cut the cabinet down to fit. The entire piece was then finished to match the new cabinets in the rest of the kitchen, resulting in a striking and unconventional display for Eisner's dazzling Fiestaware.

Although the finish work doubled the cabinet's original purchase price, it was still thousands of dollars less costly than a locally purchased cabinet would have been. The rural shop owner even threw in delivery for the price of gas.

"GUESS WHAT I FOUND?" EISNER'S BEST BARGAIN FINDS

- A salvaged legal teak veneer bookcase that is 7 feet tall and 8 feet long

- A turn-of-the-century farmhouse kitchen pantry

- A 1930s leather English pub chair and ottoman

- An oak dining table, complete with five leaves, that seats 14 people

- A pharmacy cabinet for displaying her tablecloth collection

- Aladdin lamps with opaque shades and floral bases that light up

- An oak wardrobe

- An oak Queen Anne buffet

"Once you're into the hunt, you can't help finding other great deals," says Eisner. "I love the hunt."

A One-of-a-Kind House

When the Eisners first bought their home, they emptied their cash reserves immediately with the purchase of a new furnace. That, coupled with the fact that they hate to borrow money, meant focusing their initial recovery efforts on work they could complete themselves, like painting. "That's the thing about an old house," says Eisner. "There's always skilled work that's needed, and if you don't have the skills, you have to hire the workers. It's expensive and it takes longer. We didn't anticipate how expensive."

In the following months and years, however, Eisner's talent for pursuing

This unusual front door is a vintage find that has been mounted upside down.

Creative deal-making led to a gorgeous kitchen.

rattling old panes. Last winter, they engaged a window manufacturer to custom-build 15 windows for less than $7,000 installed. The bad news is that all the windows must now be replaced—at the manufacturer's cost—because they don't fit. "One of the downsides of 'nonstandard' houses is just that," says Eisner with a shrug. "Nothing is standard."

But among the upsides is the freedom to experiment with unusual solutions. For example, the Eisners have been hunting for a salvaged front door, complete with sidelight glass and transom windows, to restore the entry's grandeur. In the meantime, they discovered two heavy wooden doors in the old stable that were original to the house. One was warped, but the other was in surprisingly good shape given its long tenure in an unheated, dirt-floor stable.

bargains has helped them make steady progress on their renovations. For example, to redesign her now-spacious new kitchen, she negotiated a favor from an architect friend for drawings. Then, to lower construction costs, she struck a deal with her contractor to complete the kitchen between his other jobs—inconveniencing the household considerably, but reducing the overall cost. And she found many of the materials herself,

from the granite countertops to the light fixtures recovered from a school demolition. "What I have to pay for someone else to do, I make up for by being a good bargain hunter," says Jan.

Replacing the windows was a tougher decision: There was little Jan could do beyond vigorous comparison-shopping to mitigate the exorbitant cost. So it took 12 years of frigid winters in the drafty house before the Eisners could afford to replace those

The door fit the entry, but the holes for the hardware didn't match the existing latch holes. So the couple turned the door upside down, filled the holes with wood filler, drilled new holes, and mounted it. The door remains unfinished "and rustic, we like to say," says Eisner. As a solution, they hope it's temporary, but it's attractive, functional, and—like everything else in and about the house—"it's unique," she says.

A Work in Progress

A dozen years of projects have barely shortened the Eisners' remodeling to-do list. Plans for future work include removing the old stable, refreshing the home's exterior with color and landscaping, replacing all the aluminum combinations, and adding gutters. Eisner has a plan for the guest room that she hopes to undertake this year. And she'd like to remove the carpeting on the first floor and install wood floors.

These and other upgrades are likely to take years, she expects, but she insists the effort and expense are worth it. "The best thing about buying an old house like this is that it has great bones, an unusual layout, and a uniqueness that makes up for a lot of the hassles of a non-standard building," she says. "Uniqueness isn't for everyone, but I love it. Like my collections, it's personal."

Part of the fun in Eisner's house is discovering unexpected items in unusual spots. Here, an antique accordian rests between two old rocking chairs.

Garden To Go

With pre-selected plants and professional planting diagrams, you can have a color-coordinated garden in a snap.

Wouldn't containers brimming with lavender and purple heliotrope, cascading orchid verbena, and trailing silver helichrysum look perfect flanking your front door? Or how about a fragrant moonlight garden filled with luminous white roses, honeysuckle, lilies, and other perennials that you could pick for bouquets? Or maybe an attractive, edible border overflowing with vividly colored Swiss chard, purple pole beans, succulent corn, red lettuce, and herbs would fit you just perfectly.

Sigh. If you only had the time—or the gardening savvy—or could find all the materials, right?

These days, you can have the gardens of your dreams without earning a doctorate in horticulture. Gardening catalogs and garden centers have recognized that some consumers just don't have the time to plan their own garden, but that those people still want something that looks nice outside.

That's why many garden companies are now selling what might be called "instant gardens" or "gardens to go."

These pre-packaged plantings might include an array of perennials, all designed to complement each other, that you can purchase at your local nursery. Tuck a planting chart under your arm, and off you go to spend a couple hours on a Saturday afternoon creating your dream garden. You can even order a pre-planned garden from a catalog. Plants or seeds and a garden diagram will be delivered to your door, just in time for weekend planting. All the decisions—which plants like the same growing conditions, what colors go together best, which plants will bloom continually—have been made for you. Your responsibility is only to put the plants in the ground or in a pot, give them a thorough watering, and stand back!

Easy fresh-flower bouquets can be as close as your garden if you make use of pre-packaged, pre-planned plantings.

What's Available in Catalogs

If you're looking for plants and plans that work well in containers, the garden merchandiser White Flower Farm has several: From the bold Summer Sensation bowls to formal urns of Silvery Elegance, these collections accent entries, decks, and walkways with little work. Summer Sensation, for example, combines sturdy annuals in strong colors such as yellow, red, and orange for non-stop blooms all season. Other container collections from White Flower Farm, such as Silvery Elegance, are good for formal settings—snapdragons in purple tones combined with deep violet vines, trailing white petunias, and silver-frosted lacy foliage. Pastel Patio, which is the heliotrope-verbena combination described in the introduction, is perfect for semi shady areas where you want continual blooms. (It's also terrific on decks or patios, since the vanilla-cherry fragrance of heliotrope is wonderful aromatherapy after a hard day.) In each collection, White Flower Farm will ship well-rooted plants that start flowering almost immediately after planting.

For large expanses of flowers, a couple of mail order catalogs offer specialty collections that are ready to plant. High Country Gardens offers

A collection of flowers from Park Nursery called The Everlasting make extraordinary bouquets.

collections perfect for low-rainfall areas of the country. These xeriscape (low water) collections also do well where the rainfall is adequate (20 to 30 inches annually). No watering is necessary in these regions once plants are established. Specialty beds include the Big Easy, a 75-square-foot expanse of brilliant red, purple, and blue water-wise flowers, and Lauren Springer's Butterfly Paradise Cottage Garden. Springer, a well-known gardener and book author, has assembled yarrow, white coneflowers, coreopsis, black-eyed Susans, and more in drifts to attract butterflies while capturing the essence of a cottage garden.

The garden company Jackson & Perkins offers large-scale deer-resistant gardens for sun and shade, plus moonlight flower beds. All collections have been selected by horticultural experts and have been planned around perennials that

will bloom from spring through fall frost. The Deer-Resistant Shade Garden, packed with colorful foliage and flowers, brightens hard-to-plant areas under trees and on the north side of structures. Perennials range in height from 12 inches to 6 feet. A diagram with numbers makes planting simple, placing the taller plants to the rear so they don't obscure the shorter flowers. Apricot foxgloves, pink pulmonaria, clear blue monkshood, and Japanese painted ferns, plus other harmonizing perennials, combine for a stunning display the deer will not touch. Another Jackson & Perkins collection is the Moonlight Shade Garden. White flowering perennials glow in the moonlight and in the shade during the day. Anemones, astilbe, phlox, forget-me-nots, hydrangea, and hostas are all delivered in a package to your door. The catalog also carries versions of the moonlight and deer-resistant gardens suitable for full-sun sites.

An Edible Border planting, offered by Nichols Garden Nursery.

The little Princess Shasta Daisy, from the Deer-Resistant Garden by Jackson & Perkins.

These foxgloves are part of a Deer-Resistant plant package offered by Jackson & Perkins.

If edibles are your dream, Nichols Garden Nursery offers the "Planting in Patterns" series. A small book, authored by Joy Larkcom, the queen of British culinary gardening, and Rose Marie Nichols-McGee, well-known herb expert, details how to plant four edible and beautiful gardens. Diagrams, detailed instructions, and recipes for the harvest are included. The expert duo use seeds to start

these gardens, as vegetables sprout and grow rapidly. A seed collection is available for each garden. The Salad Circle uses a 6-foot diameter circle that is divided with four paths for easy access. Salad herbs such as basil, dwarf marigolds, and dill are incorporated into the mix. Not only are standard salad greens such as Red and Green Salad Bowl lettuces included, but so are longer-yielding greens like perpetual spinach, Red Russian kale, and purslane. Add a couple of bush cucumber vines, and you have an attractive bed full of salad.

The Edible Border, another beautiful bed of vegetables, is detailed in the introduction. Also available are the Asian Salad Blend garden (mizuna, red mustard, pak choi, coriander, chrysanthemum greens, and more) and the Stir-Fry Plot. In this 4-by-6-foot garden, you can grow almost all the ingredients you'd ever want for stir-fry meals—garlic chives, Tatsoi, purple pak choi, mizuna, giant purple mustard, and leaf amaranth.

Park Seed Co. offers the Everlasting Collection, an Egg & Gourd Collection, and four Color Bouquet collections—all available as seeds. The Everlasting includes favorites for drying and pressing, such as Bells of Ireland, Chinese Lantern, Money

Sold as a "poached egg flower," this beauty is part of an Egg & Gourd collection by Park Seed.

Plant, and Baby's Breath. Yellow, blue, rose, and white flower mixes are available in the Color Bouquet collections. Each mix combines annuals and perennials (all bloom the first year from seed) to create a monochromatic bed that flowers at the same time. The Egg & Gourd Collection is a fun array of Easter Egg plants (a potato family ornamental), Poached Egg plants (6-inch flowers that resemble poached eggs) and Gourd Eggs, which are gourds that look exactly like hens' eggs. (Children love these!)

Planting Tips

Once a garden bed or container is planted, there is little maintenance involved, except watering. That part is critical, however. You must supply at

Also part of the Egg & Gourd collection, these decorative egg plants add whimsy to the garden.

The Summer Sensation container from White Flower Farm.

This garden is offered as a package called "The Big Easy" from High Country Gardens. It covers up to 75 square feet, and does well in dry areas.

MAIL-ORDER SOURCES

High Country Gardens
  (800) 925-9387
  www.highcountrygardens.com

Jackson & Perkins
  (800) 292-4769
  www.jacksonandperkins.com

Nichols Garden Nursery
  (800) 422-3985
  www.nicholsgardennursery.com

Park Seed Co.
  (800) 845-3369
  www.parkseed.com

White Flower Farm
  (800) 503-9624
  www.whiteflowerfarm.com

least 1 inch of water weekly to beds, unless rainfall does it for you. And containers probably need to be watered daily because pots and baskets dry out fast. Beyond that, if you plant correctly, nothing else is needed. Here is how to plant.

Select a lightweight potting mixture to fill containers. Look for sacks that are mostly peat and vermiculite.

For garden beds, don't waste your time and effort digging up the soil. Instead, mound up peat, composted manure, and bagged topsoil, and then mix them with a hoe. Spread mix in a 4-inch layer over the ground. You will create a nutrient-rich, loose soil in which plants will get a fast start. By season's end, plant roots will have softened the hard ground under-

Chinese lanterns spread easily, and are part of a plant package called The Everlasting, offered by Park Seed. (Everlasting plants dry beautifully for indoor arrangements.)

neath. Figure on one 3.6-cubic-foot bale of peat moss, two 40-pound sacks of manure, and four 40-pound bags of topsoil for each 10 square feet.

Use gradual-release fertilizers that feed plants for 90 days or more. The brand Osmocote, for instance, will provide a steady amount of nutrients to plants for three months. Incorporate fertilizer with soil in garden beds and in containers before planting. Amounts needed will be listed on fertilizer packages.

To simplify watering tasks, wind a soaker hose through garden beds, and a twist of the water faucet handle is all the labor you'll need when watering. Use a timer to further automate this chore. Water containers and hanging baskets when the soil is dry 1 inch under the surface. (Push your index finger up to its first joint into the dirt. If your fingertip is dry, water; if it's damp, don't.)

Finally, mulch beds to stop soil moisture from evaporating and you won't have to water as often. Cover the ground with 2 to 3 inches of shredded bark, pine needles, compost, or shredded leaves. (Cover soaker hoses with mulch as well to capture all their moisture.)

Wallpaper Secrets

These simple tricks and tips make applying wallpaper a smooth job.

Painting a room is easy— all you need are a brush, a roller, and a bucket of paint. Installing wallcovering is another story. It's sticky and wet and involves math skills and sharp tools. People who try it seem to end up in one of two camps: either they think it's great fun and look forward to the next opportunity, or they are permanently scarred and have the divorce papers to prove it.

That's why hanging wallcovering is the ultimate do-it-yourself project— because in some cases, it's best to do it (all by) your-self. Those who accept the challenge will reap the benefits of added color, dimension, personality, and style. Although a wallcovering project has more potential for frustration than painting does, you can avoid some of the pitfalls before your hands are even wet (see "Boost Your Odds of Success," on Page 132). In the end, you can achieve attractive results provided you have a good strategy, accurate information, the right equipment, and a little patience.

How Much Paper Should I Buy?

Wallcovering is packaged in double rolls, usually containing about 56 square feet of paper. (Note that prices are marked for single rolls.) To determine how much you'll need, multiply each wall's height by its width to figure the square footage of the wall surface. Do the same with all doors and windows and then subtract those numbers from your total square footage.

Once you've done this, the easiest way to figure quantity is to take those numbers to the store where you've selected your wallpaper and ask an expert there to help you decide how much paper to buy. (Waste from matching the pattern and other factors will affect the actual usable yield.)

If you've never hung wallpaper before, do yourself a favor and select an inexpensive wallcovering rather than a pricey one for your first project. That way, you won't see dollar signs whenever you have to recut or rehang a strip. But don't skimp on quantity. If you allow room for errors, they're less likely to happen.

For this makeover project, our bedroom was 11 by 14 feet with 9-foot ceilings. We subtracted the square footage of our three doors and four windows to find our final number. The wallcovering we selected, which was in the Antique Chic line made by Seabrook, had a 21-inch pattern match, so we bought eight double rolls, allowing for waste and a little extra in case of mishaps.

Preparing the Room

As with painting, proper preparation saves time and helps prevent accidents. Use drop cloths, turn off the room's power, remove electrical plates and ventilation covers, and cover outlets with masking tape.

Remove any existing wallcovering and paste residue. I always try to first dry-peel the strips (or at least the top layer) by gently pulling the paper off the wall in large sections. If that doesn't work, or if a paper backing remains on the wall, use steam or a liquid stripper such as Dif to soften the adhesive, then peel or scrape the paper off the wall with a putty knife.

If you find that the wallcovering still doesn't strip easily, score the outer layer of the paper with a tool such as the Paper Tiger (see our Special Tip at the bottom of Page 134). The serrated teeth on this tool will "bite" into the paper, leaving hundreds of tiny holes in the wallcovering. You can then proceed with steam or a liquid stripper, which will penetrate the paper more efficiently.

Once you've removed the wallcovering, wash the walls with a diluted solution of Dif or a mild detergent, then rinse and let dry.

Next, patch and prime holes and dents. If you plan to paint the ceiling and trim, do that now.

Whether the walls were previously papered or painted, always apply wall sizing. This crucial coating makes the wall surface compatible with the paste and new wallcovering. The strips will slide into position easily and hold in place more readily. And in the future, when the wallcovering is removed, it will easily separate from the wall.

If the walls have never been painted, such as with new Sheetrock, it's an excellent idea to apply a product such as Shieldz, manufactured by Zinsser (about $17 a gallon), that primes and sizes in one step.

AFTER

BEFORE

Installation

Because the starting and ending wallpaper edges will almost never have a perfect pattern match, start your first strip in an inconspicuous corner. Draw a plumb line to align the right edge of your first strip, allowing an extra $\frac{1}{2}$ inch or so to wrap around the corner. Regardless of ceiling sags, crooked corners or other misalignments in the room, the wallcovering strips must be perfectly vertical. You'll need to start with a plumb line on each new wall as well.

To cut the length of wallpaper strips, measure the height of the wall and add 4 inches for trimming (2 inches at each end). Plan ahead to avoid having a large pattern element or obvious horizontal line end at the ceiling. After you've successfully installed the first strip, cut the next few strips, watching for pattern matches and allowing for waste at both ends. You will develop a rhythm for cutting, pasting, and hanging as you go; work steadily so the previous strip doesn't dry completely before you hang the next one. Take breaks at the corners, where it's easier to start with a wet strip next to one that is dry.

About 15 minutes after hanging each strip, set the seam with a single, light run of a seam roller. Do not press hard or you will push the paste away from the seams. Wash paste residue off each strip and the surrounding surfaces as you go. Once paste dries, it's nearly impossible to remove.

Wallcovering projects involve an element of luck—and some creative problem solving. Experience teaches tricks and techniques you can't learn from any article. But with each room you transform, the satisfaction you feel will be a tremendous reward.

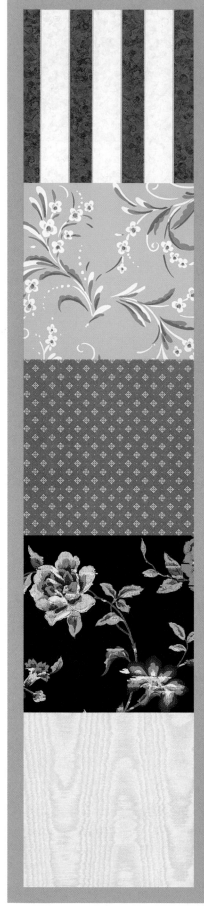

BOOST YOUR ODDS OF SUCCESS

If you're a first-time paperhanger, you can minimize frustration by taking these measures:

Choose the right project. Don't be fooled into thinking that a small area such as a bathroom is a good beginner project. Bathrooms can be daunting because they have numerous obstacles (towel bars, toilets, etc.) and very little uninterrupted wall surface. Likewise, kitchens with small sections of wall space are not as innocent as they may seem. And though large entryways or stairwells have greater wall areas, they are difficult because they involve angled ceilings, longer strips of wallcovering and a lot of ladder time.

Choose the best product. Some wallcoverings are more cooperative than others, and though you can't fully predict their workability until you're already committed, you can avoid some hassles by making careful selections. For example, buy patterns with light backgrounds. If the seams separate even by a hair (and some will), they will be distractingly obvious if the wall color greatly contrasts with the paper's background color. In addition, strong geometric patterns demand perfect matching and alignment of corners. Conversely, a paper with a random, flowing pattern can work to your advantage by disguising slight surface imperfections, crooked corners, and wavy ceilings.

Use quality adhesive. The dry adhesives on today's prepasted wallcoverings are very reliable. Still, it doesn't hurt to have some ready-mixed adhesive on hand in case an edge dries a bit during the handling time. Don't be afraid to buy an unpasted wall-covering—it's not difficult to apply paste with a roller, and you can control the amount that goes on. Just be sure to buy washable vinyl or vinyl-coated wallcovering—leave natural-fiber and specialty wallcoverings to the pros.

Choose the right process. The usual surface-preparation criteria (clean, dry, smooth, etc.) are important, but never skip the critical step of applying sizing to the walls. It makes installation (and eventual removal) of wallcovering so much easier.

Use the right equipment. All do-it-yourselfers know that the right equipment is essential. Keep a sharp blade on your cutting tool. I like the Olfa standard cutter with snap-off blades. Use a sturdy ladder and have a smoother, a straightedge, scissors, etc., accessible. Work when you have energy and time; you'll have more patience. And finally—no, firstly—read the instructions that come with the wallcovering. Note the recommended soaking time and water temperature for prepasted papers, recommended adhesives for unpasted, and booking time for both. Those details vary from product to product.

To Wallpaper Like the Pros You Will Need:

◆ Sizing for walls (this paint-like product makes wallpaper application and later removal much easier)
◆ Pencil and/or chalk line
◆ Tape measure and ruler
◆ Wallpaper
◆ Sharp knife
◆ Paper smoothing tool
◆ Water tray for soaking paper

1 Start your wallcovering project in a corner. Lightly draw a plumb line to align the right-hand edge of the first strip. Our line is no more than 19¼ inches from the corner (check in three locations) to allow the 20½-inch-wide paper to wrap tightly into the corner. Note: Using a chalk line is an easy way to create a straight line, but be careful not to smear the chalk onto the paper when attaching the wallcovering. We created a chalk line first and then gently wiped off most of the chalk BEFORE we placed our wet paper on the wall to minimize this.

2 When cutting wallpaper to size for a wall, remember to leave an extra 2 inches of paper at both the top and bottom for trimming. We found it easiest to work with two rolls of paper at a time, stretched carefully over a long table. That way, we could adjust the strips to find the pattern match and then cut the pieces.

3 Loosely roll the strip, pasted side out, and dip it into a tray of water that is positioned under the drip edge of a work surface. (Check the manufacturer's instructions for water temperature and dipping time.) As you slowly draw the strip from the water, make sure there are no dry areas.

Fold each end toward the center of the strip, pasted sides together. Gently roll the strip, being careful not to crease the folds. Giving the paste a short time to activate and the paper a time to soften this way is called "booking." Book the strip for the time recommended by the manufacturer before you apply it to the wall.

Open the top half of the strip and position it about ⅛ inch to the left of your plumb line. Gently smooth the upper half of the strip, checking that the right edge stays even with the plumb line and the left edge reaches around the corner. Open the lower half of the strip and continue to position the paper with your hand.

4 Once the strip is in place, use a smoother to eliminate large air bubbles. Don't overwork the paper. Small bubbles will disappear as the paste dries.

5 Keeping the 2-inch waste off the ceiling, crease firmly into the wall/ceiling edge with a flat tool designed for use with wallpaper.

With a sharp razor blade or a utility knife, gently cut along the straight-edge. It doesn't take much pressure to split existing drywall joint tape, so be careful. Trim along the baseboard in the same way. Wipe paste residue off the baseboard and the wallcovering.

After dipping and booking the second strip, open and hang the top half first, matching any pattern elements and positioning it so the seams (edges) are butted tightly but not overlapped. Be careful not to pull or stretch the paper because it will shrink back to its relaxed state as it dries.

To create tightly wrapped corners and hang perfectly vertical strips, make a seam in each corner. Measure the greatest distance from the last strip to the corner and add ½ inch. After soaking and booking a full strip, cut this width off the left edge of the strip and hang it, wrapping the ½ inch excess tightly into the corner. Draw a plumb line on the next wall according to the width of the remaining strip. Apply vinyl adhesive along the area of the overlap.

SPECIAL TIP

If you can't easily peel off an existing wallcovering, pierce the nonporous vinyl layer with a scoring tool such as the Paper Tiger. (Press lightly.) Sharp teeth on swiveling wheels make it easy to puncture the surface so steam or a stripping product can penetrate to the adhesive.

Tiger's teeth

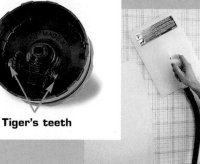

6 At a door or window, position the strip as far as possible, butting seams and matching patterns. Crease into the vertical frame and cut a miter to the corner of the frame. Smooth and crease the section of the strip that is above the frame and trim with the straightedge and knife. Again, wash the woodwork and wallcovering.

7 When you come to an electrical box or wall socket, verify that the power is off. Position the strip as flat as possible on the wall. Cut diagonally from one corner of the box to the opposite corner and again in the opposite direction to create an "X" over the area of the box. Finish smoothing the strip around the obstacle; then cut along the edges of the electrical box.

8 A seam roller is a small hand tool you can use to ensure that your seams are tightly sealed. Press lightly but firmly as you draw the roller down the seams once. Do not overwork seams or you will push the paste out of the area. Gently wipe down the seams after rolling using a slightly damp cloth.

Storing Toys

If you want a clever way to store stuffed toys, or a romantic floral accent piece, a decorative screen fits the bill.

Traditionally, decorative folding screens were produced for practical purposes—they were used to provide privacy or to serve as protection from drafts or strong sun.

Today, however, folding screens can be much more than a utilitarian part of a room. They can serve as both a practical and decorative accessory in any setting.

Creating a decorative screen is surprisingly easy, and the choices you make for fabric, trim, and accessories let you personalize this project your way.

This version is lightweight and constructed over a wood 2-by-2 framework. A romantic version of the screen, appropriate for adults, is covered with a floral fabric. A fun version, designed especially for use in a child's room, serves double-duty as a colorful storage spot for stuffed animals.

A few notes before you start: In order to complete this project, you will need ample space and a large table. A workbench is helpful, but not entirely necessary. The basic structure for each screen panel consists of two sides and four crossbars, one for the top and bottom and two evenly spaced in between. You can design your wall screens with four panels, but if you have limited space, your wall screen can be reduced to three panels.

When choosing your covering fabric, there are a few things you will want to consider: For example, striped fabric can present a challenge for covering wall screens because the fabric lines can be difficult to keep straight when stapling the material to the frame. If you are using florals or fabrics that have a distinctive repeat, you may require additional fabric to match. If you will be constructing the stuffed animal screen, choose a sturdy fabric such as a medium-weight cotton or upholstery fabric—not an open or loosely woven material—so that the weight of the toys will not stretch the fabric.

To Create a Wall Screen You Will Need:

- ◆ Several pieces of 8-foot, 2-by-2 wood (8 for child's screen; 10 for traditional screen)
- ◆ Measuring tape
- ◆ Saw
- ◆ Sandpaper
- ◆ Drill & $7/64$ drill bit, $1/4$-inch drill bit (child's screen only)
- ◆ Screwdriver
- ◆ One box No. 6, $2\frac{1}{4}$-inch fine thread drywall screws
- ◆ 16 'L' brackets with 1-inch screws
- ◆ (Child's screen:) 7 yards, medium-weight fabric, 54 inches wide: (Traditional screen:) 9 yards, 54 inches wide
- ◆ Decorative remnant fabrics (child's screen only)
- ◆ Staple gun
- ◆ 3 packages—$3/8$-inch staples
- ◆ Hot-glue gun
- ◆ Decorative trim (16 yards for child's screen;19 yards traditional screen)
- ◆ Three pairs $1\frac{1}{8}$-inch double-action hinges*
- ◆ Four wood shelf brackets
- ◆ **Optional:** Decorative finials, dowels, and wood glue

Screen dimensions are: Stuffed animal screen—each panel is 60-by-18 inches (4 panels);

Traditional screen—each panel is 72-by-18 (4 panels)

*These hinges allow two-way movement of the screen panels and are available at woodworking or home improvement stores.

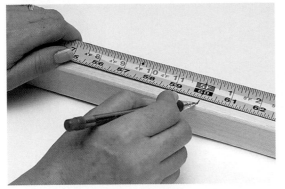

1 Measure and mark cuts on 2-by-2 pieces. For the child's screen, you will need 8 pieces that are 60 inches long (for the sides) and 16 pieces that are 15 inches long (for crossbars). For the traditional screen, cut 8 pieces 72 inches long and 16 pieces 15 inches long. Tip: To save time, mark all your measurements first and then cut.

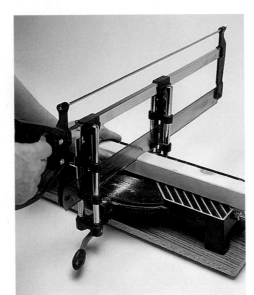

2 Cut all pieces. It is important to keep your cuts square to ensure the stability of the wall screen. (If you are using a traditional hand saw, you may find it is difficult to keep your cuts level. Using a miter saw to cut the 2-by-2 solves this problem. If you are comfortable with power tools, this step proceeds much faster using a power saw.)

Sand any rough edges on the wood that may create snags or tears in your fabric.

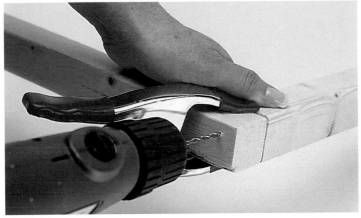

3 To assemble the frames, start by securing the top and bottom crossbar to one side of the frame. Using a ⁷⁄₆₄ drill bit, drill 2 pilot holes through length of sidepiece into crossbar. Tip: Using a clamp to hold both pieces in place is helpful.

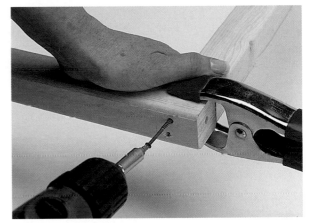

4 Screw crossbars in place at top and bottom and repeat steps 3 and 4 on opposite side.

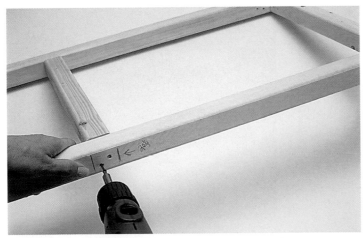

5 Evenly space additional crossbars in frame and secure in place following the same procedure used with the top and bottom crossbars. Repeat steps 3 through 5 to complete the remaining 3 frames.

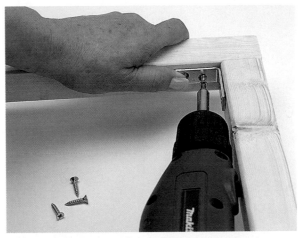

6 Attach 'L' brackets in all 4 corners of each frame. This step adds stability to the frame.

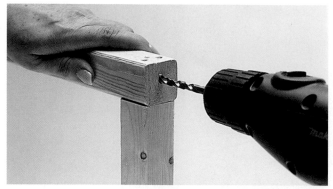

7 (Optional) Using ¼-inch drill bit, pre-drill pilot holes in the corner of each frame for decorative finials, if you plan to add these. (The finials will be attached after the screen is covered by fabric.) Tip: Pre-drill both the top and bottom corners of each frame. This way, you won't have to remember which is the top or bottom of the screen once the fabric covers the frame.

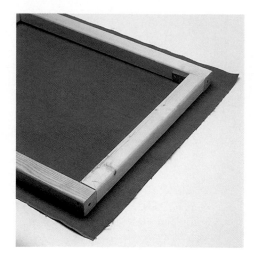

8 Measure and cut fabric 3 inches wider and 3 inches longer than the actual frame. (For example, the child's screen frames measure 60 inches by 18 inches, so the fabric was cut 63 inches by 21 inches. Cut 8 pieces of fabric to size, one for the front and back of each frame. (Tip: Keep fabric cuts square to make it easier to line up the material with the frame in a later step.)

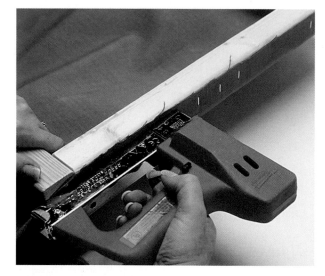

9 Center a frame over a piece of fabric. Starting at one end of the frame, keeping the edge of the fabric even with the edge of the frame, staple fabric in place. Start in the center of a top or bottom piece and move out toward the sides. Keep staples about ½ inch apart. Once fabric is secured in place, add additional staples to hold the fabric firmly. Staples should almost touch along the frame.

10 Repeat step 9, stapling the fabric to one side of each frame.

11 Starting at opposite end of frame pull the fabric taut with one hand, and staple fabric in place with the other. Start in the middle and work out to each side, repeating the procedure used in Step 9. It is important to get the fabric as taut as possible. Tip: This step can be easier if you have a helper to stretch or staple with you.

12 Trim away any excess fabric. The raw edge of the fabric should just cover the edge of the frame. Repeat steps 9 through 12 for each panel. You have now completed the back sides of your decorative screen.

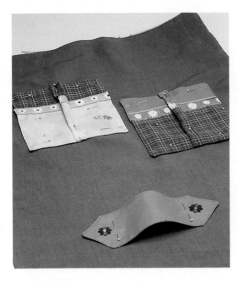

13 If you are making the traditional screen, proceed to Step 15.

If you are making the child's screen, at this point place and pin decorative pockets to the unmounted fabric for the front of each panel. (See page 140 for pocket instructions.) Use several pins to keep pockets in place, as you will be moving the fabric around while sewing the pockets down. Tip: Remember that your fabric is 3 inches wider than the frame. Keep placement of pockets at least 4 inches in from outside edges of fabric.

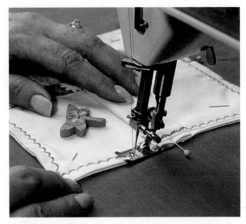

14 Sew pockets in place, lining up outside edge of pocket with outside edge of sewing foot.

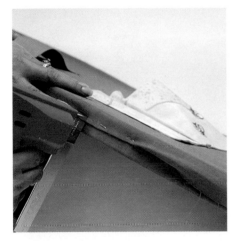

15 Staple the face fabric to the frame using the same method as for the back side. Turn the raw edge of the fabric under before stapling to the frame to conceal raw edges. Place all staples vertically, keeping the folded edge of the fabric as close to the middle of the frame as possible. This will ensure that the trim covers the staples and is in the middle of the frame. Tip: Staple the fabric to the top of the frame and then proceed to the bottom frame piece, leaving sides unstapled for the moment. This will help to keep the fabric straight. Follow with the sides, always working from the center out toward the ends.

16 Hot-glue trim to frame. Work in 6- to 8-inch sections, and start at the bottom of one side piece. Do not put trim across the bottom of the panel, as it will affect the screen's stability.

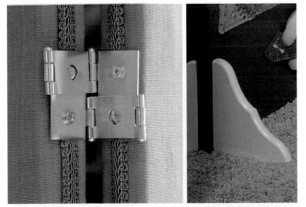

17 Attach hinges 12 inches from the top and bottom of one frame. Place a second frame beside the first, ensuring tops and bottoms are even. Attach the hinge to the second frame, following manufacturer's directions. Repeat with remaining frames. (Note: For additional stability, screw two wooden shelf brackets to the front and back of panels 1 and 4 of the child's screen.)

OPTION: ADD FINIALS

Using a ¼-inch drill bit, drill a ¾-inch hole in bottom of each finial. Use wood glue to put wood dowels in place. Let dry and then paint in a coordinating color. Use a pin to locate the pre-drilled hole in the top of the frame. Pierce through the fabric with an awl. Attach finials to the frame. If finials are loose, add a dab of wood glue to keep them in place. Tip: Move the trim toward the front of the frame rather than trying to pierce through it.

DECORATIVE POCKET DIRECTIONS

Our decorative pockets consisted of three pieces of fabric—a front, a back, and a decorative cuff—all sewn together into a flat piece of cloth. (A pocket is created by sewing this piece of cloth to the panel fabric.) We also created simple fabric "tabs" to hold small toys. Iron-on appliques and decorative buttons are easy and inexpensive embellishments for all these pieces. Plan your pockets on graph paper before moving to the screen. Done to scale, this will save you time (and money!) as it helps to determine the number of pockets needed to complete your project.

Pattern Guide for Pockets

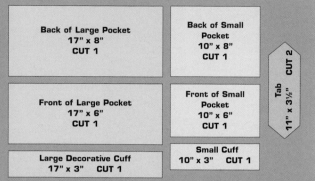

Back of Large Pocket
17" x 8"
CUT 1

Back of Small Pocket
10" x 8"
CUT 1

Front of Large Pocket
17" x 6"
CUT 1

Front of Small Pocket
10" x 6"
CUT 1

Large Decorative Cuff
17" x 3"   CUT 1

Small Cuff
10" x 3"   CUT 1

Tab
11" x 3½"   CUT 2

Our screen consisted of 6 large pockets, 13 small pockets, and 7 tabs. Note: Each pocket has one or two "pleats" in the front to create a pouch for the stuffed animals to sit in (see Steps 4 and 5).

1 With right sides together, sew decorative cuff to top, front side of pocket using ½-inch seam allowance. Press seam open.

2 With right sides together, sew front of pocket to back of pocket, leaving a small opening to turn pocket right side out. Press.

3 Attach decorative trim to front side of pocket using seam line on decorative cuff as a guide for placement. Iron on appliques or decorative buttons add a wonderful finishing touch, but are not necessary.

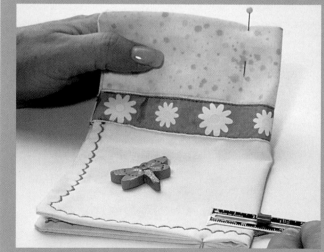

4 In order for the toys to fit in the pockets, you need to create a pleat at the bottom edge to make a pouch. (Large pockets need two pleats, one on either side of center.) Fold small pocket in half and place pin 1 inch from folded edge at top and bottom of pocket.

5 Lay the pocket flat and fold fabric down to create a small pleat. Sew in place. Leave pin in at top of pocket until after you have attached the pocket to panel fabric. (This keeps the pocket square when attaching it. See Step 13 on page 139.)

Ceiling Medallion

Have you ever walked into a grand old home and fallen in love with the small details around light fixtures? These medallions are raised, textured, decorative elements that accentuate the beauty of those old fixtures.

Today it's possible to capture the look of those ceiling medallions for very little work, and at a reasonable price. Several companies make medallions that can be added to a home to enhance ceilings, but a new product from a company called Style Solutions, based in Archbold, Ohio, makes the installation process literally a "snap."

Style Solution's new two-piece ceiling medallions interlock around the base of most light fixtures or ceiling fans. Made of lightweight urethane that can be painted or stained, the two-piece product fits together like two pieces of a jigsaw puzzle, locking into place around the base of the fixture. This means users don't have to dismantle existing light fixtures to add this element to a room, and can complete installation quickly.

"There's no quicker way to add a decorative element to a room than our new two-piece ceiling medallions," says Mike Reed, director of marketing for Style Solutions, Inc. "This is a one-person job that easily transforms the look of a room in minutes."

One other unique feature of these medallions is that the surface of the piece can be painted or faux-finished to match any decor. Users can also highlight the medallions with other techniques, such as adding gold leaf or marblelizing to the piece before installing it.

To install these medallions, users simply shut off the electrical breaker that controls the ceiling fan or light fixture concerned. Using standard screws, users space the screws at regular intervals part way through the front of the medallion, staying 1 or 2 inches from the edge. (Screws can be placed in the detailed portion of the medallion to hide them after installation.)

Then a special millwork adhesive is applied to the back portion of the medallion, and each half of the medallion is fit into place around the fixture. Once the medallion is in place, the screws can be countersunk through the piece into the ceiling. Extra adhesive can be wiped off with a clean cloth, if necessary. That's all there is to it.

Style Solutions is introducing four designs of medallions for 2002, ranging from contemporary to classic. The introductory designs are called Bridgeport, Chelsea, Lenox, and Florentine.

Prices for the medallions range from $35 to about $65, depending on size and style.

To find a dealer near you, call (800) 446-3040.

Chapter four
How-To

Sometimes the only thing separating you from craft and decorating success is a little know-how. These quick, easy and fun ideas will inspire you!

How To...
Make Your Own Tags and Bags

As the season for gift giving approaches, why not turn your creative energies to making the outside of your presents as special as the inside?

It's easy to do and (in some cases) is less expensive than choosing "store-bought" wrappings, bows, and cards. And it goes without saying that a personalized gift is more special to the recipient.

Making gift cards or tags can be as simple or as complex as you choose. You'll find that making several items of a similar type saves time and money once you start your project. A few items that prove helpful no matter what style tag you want to make include:

- **Rubber stamps and pads.** Use one stamp or a selection to create a theme on a card, such as reindeer and snowflakes or simple leaf patterns done in metallic tones.

- **Embossing powder and an embossing gun** (both let you create "raised" designs on your tags by heating the powder to make it puff up). These can be used alone or with stamps or stencils.

- **A variety of acrylic craft paints** and brushes will let you add highlights to a card, perhaps creating a fanciful face for your Santa stamp, or picking out veins and stems on a leaf stencil.

- **Glitter glue sticks**, gold and silver pens, and rolls of decorative ribbon in your workbasket will let you add a finishing touch to any tag.

There are a wide variety of decorative papers available in any craft shop, but let your imagination guide you. You can also make tags from old sheet music, leftover wall coverings, conventional wrapping or tissue paper, or any other material that can be embellished.

Once you've created a personalized tag, why not make a coordinating bag? A super-simple way to do this is by appliqueing fabric cutouts onto a colored bag.

To do this, you'll need paper bags, seasonal fabric with bright designs, double-sided fusible webbing (one brand is sold as "Wonder-Under Transfer Web" by Pellon), glitter glue sticks, and gold and silver pens.

Press your fabric to remove any wrinkles. Choose part of the pattern from the fabric to use as the image on your gift bag. Roughly cut around the pattern.

Apply double-sided fusible web to the wrong side of fabric following manufacturer's instructions. Let cool and peel off paper backing. (Note: Manufacturer's instructions say to cut out the pattern and then remove the paper backing. We found it easier to get a clean edge by removing the paper backing first and then cutting around the pattern.) Position the cut out on the gift bag, cover with a cotton cloth and press in place.

Choose fabrics that have a combination of large and small elements. That way, you can even make a matching appliqued tag for your bag.

How To...
Create a Silk Orchid Display

Orchids add a burst of color to any winter-bound home. These lovely, tropical plants bloom for several months given proper care, and add a delicate, nodding form to any table or dresser top.

Real orchids require only a few special conditions to look their best. However, in some cases, the room where you want to place an orchid doesn't offer the right light, or you aren't able to meet some of the plant's other needs. That's where a silk orchid display works beautifully.

If you haven't paid a visit to your local hobby or craft store lately to inspect the newest generation of silk flowers, you're in for a surprise. Today's silks are almost indistinguishable from real. Better yet, they maintain their beauty with little more than an occasional dusting, and they aren't bothered by drafts or an erratic or nonexistent watering schedule.

You can buy pre-made silk orchid arrangements in dozens of stores, but you'll pay a premium for them. We saw some simple displays like the one shown here for $70 and more. We re-created the same look in less than half an hour with a few simple items, and one beautiful silk orchid that we purchased ourselves for about $10.

To do this, you'll need a terra-cotta pot or other decorative container about one-third as tall as your orchid stem. You'll also need some inexpensive green floral foam, and a bag of dried sphagnum moss, both readily available at any craft store. (You may want to throw in a few decorative pebbles, as well.)

Simply cut your floral foam to fit inside the base of your container. Some silk orchids come with a base of three green leaves attached, and these look the most realistic in a container. You can pull off the base of leaves—which are simply pressed around the orchid stem—and then cut the stem to the length you want. Press the leaves securely into the center of the foam, and thread the orchid stem back inside the leaf base. Arrange sphagnum moss around the base of the orchid to conceal the floral foam. Finish with a few decorative pebbles on top of the moss, if you wish.

Orchids look most natural when the floral stems are bent slightly outward. You can use a piece of string or a green twist tie to secure the stems at the angle you wish.

How To...
Create a "Seasonal" Lamp Shade

When the garden is in full bloom, it's tempting to pick an armful of flowers every day.

That temptation inspired this fun "temporary" lamp shade that you can embellish to suit every season. The flower-packed shade is actually a slip-cover of sorts for an everyday lamp.

To do this, you'll need a lamp with an existing shade, about a yard of plastic sheeting from your local sewing store, several bunches of inexpensive silk flowers, and a hot-glue gun.

The plastic sheeting we used for this shade comes in a variety of weights, and we found ours for about $1.50 a yard at our local sewing goods store. Choose a heavier weight of sheeting for this project. The sheeting generally comes with backing paper that you can use to create a paper pattern for your lamp cover (or simply use a large sheet of thin, white paper to make your pattern).

Remove your lamp shade from the lamp and lay it seam-side down on your paper. Make a mark at the top and the bottom of the shade where the seam falls. Then simply roll your shade slowly across the paper, and continue marking top and bottom until you have "C"-shaped pattern of the shade itself. Carefully cut around this paper pattern, remove the cut piece, and place it around your shade to check for fit. Make any adjustments necessary so that the paper pattern fits the shade well. Trace your pattern onto the plastic, leaving an extra half-inch or so at each end of the pattern to overlap. Place the plastic over your existing shade and carefully hot-glue the overlapping ends together.

It's easiest to hot-glue the silk flower heads to this shade if the plastic is on the existing shade and the existing shade is on the lamp. Separate the heads from several bunches of silk flowers and then, working carefully, begin to glue these to the plastic shade. Set your glue gun at its coolest setting, and watch carefully to make sure you don't melt the plastic or get glue on your original shade. Work in rows from the bottom of the shade up, and fill in any sparse areas with a few smaller flowers.

That's all there is to it. You can slip this flower shade on and off whenever you want, or you can create several different versions to match the seasons.

How To...
Paint a Colorful Mural

Adding a colorful mural to a wall adds tremendous impact to any room, especially a child's. However, tackling such a project can be daunting for "non-painters."

A product called Wall Art offers a nifty solution to that dilemma: The product is a paint-by-numbers kit that comes complete with one of 75 ready-made, large-sized, kid-friendly mural themes printed on tracing paper, ready to transfer to any size wall. (See image below.)

Wall Art murals come in three standard sizes—5-by-3 feet, 9-by-5 feet, and an extra-large 11½-by-6½ feet. However, the mural designs are flexible enough to be trimmed to fit odd-sized spaces. Each mural kit contains step-by-step instructions, a suggested paint guide to match the image, tracing pencil, paintbrush, and tape. Prices range from $25 for smaller murals up to $50 for the largest size.

Wall Art murals work well on any light-colored smooth wall surface. Users position the mural on the wall, tape it in place, and then trace over the preprinted image. (See photo at bottom left.) A colored tracing pencil makes it easy to see which areas have been completed. After the image has been transferred to the wall, users remove the paper and tape and can begin painting.

An accompanying color guide offers suggestions for selecting and using paint for each particular mural. Small, 2-ounce bottles of acrylic paint (not included) are recommended for most mural designs, although some larger areas may require slightly more paint. However, users can adapt the suggested color scheme by selecting different shades that better match their own decor.

A special slant-edged brush is included in the kit to help fill in the sections, but the painting process is a forgiving one: Slight imperfections in each area can be camouflaged by drawing over the image with an outlining pen for a clean, crisp line once the sections have been painted.

The company that manufactures Wall Art murals, HDA Inc., suggests that users paint light colors and larger areas of the murals first, and then move on to smaller details. Other embellishments, including colored paint markers or glitter or glow-in-the-dark paint, are more options that let users customize their images to their own tastes.

For more information, or to see mural designs available, call (877) WALL-MURAL [(877) 925-5687] or visit www.muralsbywallart.com. Wall Art murals are also available at Hobby Lobby, Do it Best, and Lowe's stores.

PAINT-BY-NUMBER
Follow the easy Paint-by-Number pattern below to create the design as shown.
Except for your base coat, most colors require 2 ozs., larger areas require 4 ozs.

How To...
Choose Color

Considering its impact, paint is the cheapest decorating project you can pursue. A few dollars, a few hours, and you can change the entire impact of a room.

But paint—or more appropriately, color—can intimidate some of us. We may have always secretly wanted a bright red room with bright yellow accents, but what if we try it and don't like it? Or our family doesn't like it? Or what if our friends think we're crazy?

That indecision can leave us afraid of making any choice.

But there are ways to gauge the effect of our decisions before lifting a brush. People who specialize in the science

(and emotion) of color agree that certain colors evoke certain moods—soft yellows, oranges, and reds are cozy and warm; bright greens are cheerful and energizing; pale pastels are calm and quiet.

Decide why you want to try a new color. Do you have an heirloom rug you'd like to update with a complementary color? Would you like to feature an unusual sofa by placing it against a contrasting wall? (Or would you rather de-emphasize it by choosing a color that makes it almost disappear?)

Don't be afraid to consult a pro if you're still unsure. Many interior designers and color consultants will rent themselves out by the hour to help with your plans. At their best, pros can open your eyes to options you'd never imagined. At the very least, such advisers can confirm your own instincts.

Pick a color or two that you like and then explore this idea further using a color wheel. You may remember the color wheel from school—it's usually a round piece of plastic that has a graduated spectrum of colors built around the primaries of red, blue, and yellow. Understanding the relationships of color can become much clearer with a color wheel in hand.

For example, when you combine two of the primary colors in equal measure, you get a secondary color: red and yellow become orange; red and blue become violet; and blue and yellow become green. Combine these colors with the primary color adjacent on the wheel and you get the six tertiary colors: red and orange become red-orange; red and violet become red-violet; and so on, stretching as far as your imagination can take you. Adding white to a color creates a tint, adding black creates a shade, and adding gray creates a tone. The differences are called values, and these account for the hundreds and thousands of different colors you can order in a paint store. Balancing values is key to making your color choices work. For example, a room with only dark colors will feel gloomy, while one that uses only pale tints may feel bland.

The emotional or sensory properties of the colors on either side of the wheel can also overwhelm you unless they're balanced. For example, half the color wheel contains reds, yellows, and oranges. These colors advance—meaning they can create an effect of coziness that can become claustrophobic without cooler colors for relief. On the other half of a color wheel are the cool colors—the blues and greens—which are said to recede and can make a room seem larger: Such opposites—the cool versus the warm—are complements that, when used together, help you achieve a pleasing balance.

ILLUSTRATION OF COLOR RELATIONSHIPS

How To...
Mix and Match Fabrics

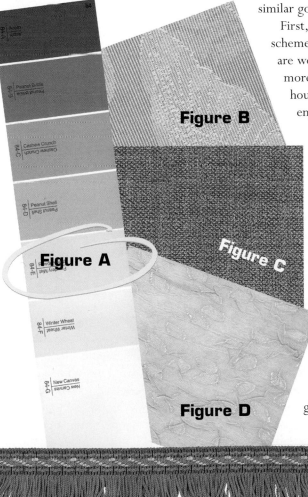

Figure A

Figure B

Figure C

Figure D

Look around any home, and you'll find a glorious mixture of colors, shapes, furniture, and decorative objects. In a home that fits its inhabitants perfectly, this mix is one that brings pleasure to all of the senses.

There is another way to enhance the "sensory" pleasure of any home for a small amount of cash, by mixing and matching different fabric textures and colors into a complementary whole.

Texture—and color—were all criteria for selecting fabrics that worked together to create a cohesive look. Along the way, we discovered a few hints that may help you pursue a similar goal.

First, consider the overall color scheme of the area in which you are working. Do you spend more daylight hours or evening hours in the space? Do you enjoy the serene look of a monochromatic color scheme or does the "pow" of bright colors make you feel more at home?

If you have a paint chip of your room or a favorite fabric swatch, lay the material on a sheet of white paper and study it. You'll find that any shade of paint or fabric has hints of other base colors in it—say a green shade that shows a suggestion of yellow, or a light blue that actually has a slightly gray appearance.

Keeping in mind the color of the room, we moved to our largest fabric purchase—the slipcover material (see Figure B). This rosy-beige, lightweight upholstery fabric with a faint white outline of raised leaves blended well with the room color.

To select outside panels for the curtains (the next most dominant color in the room), we selected a fluid polyester material with a visible "grain," in a rich brown with rosy-beige and almond undertones (see Figure C).

The next largest fabric purchase was the sheers. We found an almond-toned silky material in a "crunchy" fabric that also had small "leaf" shapes in it, which softly echoed the leaves on the upholstery fabric and blended harmoniously with the other colors (see Figure D).

If you can do all of your fabric shopping in one day, as we did, you'll find that nothing beats holding bolts of cloth next to each other to see the interplay of colors and textures. You'll find that cottons can work beautifully with polyester blends, or that upholstery-weight material can mingle elegantly with silks.

How To...
Choose a Lamp Shade

Choosing the right shade for a favorite lamp can offer the crowning touch to any room. Unfortunately, it's also true that choosing the wrong size or color shade can sound a sour note in any melodious decorating scheme.

There are more choices of lamp shades available now than ever before. For a few dollars, you can add color, pattern, height, weight, and visual interest to any part of a room, often changing the entire look of an area without much effort.

A perfect time to consider a new shade is when you are changing the colors in a room, perhaps changing from the darker, warmer colors of winter to the cooler, lighter colors preferred in spring.

Here are a few tips to help you choose the perfect shade for any lamp.

- **Size:** A well-fitted shade should just skim the top of the lamp base. There are a number of fittings you can purchase at any decorating or home furnishing store that will help you do this. A harp is generally made of flexible metal, with two bottom "feet" that fit around the socket of the lamp. The shade attaches to the top of this harp with a screw. Fine-tune the height of your shade by changing the size of the harp or by adding a riser (which fits inside the shade to give extra height). Keep in mind the propor-

tions of the lamp when selecting a shade. A small lamp that is overpowered by a large shade does not look as well as one that is balanced when it comes to "visual weight."

- **Shape:** Choose a shade that complements the shape of the lamp. If you have a fat-bellied vintage lamp, consider a warm, softly rounded shade that will enhance that effect. However, if you have a sleek, modern lamp, a shade with strong, clean lines might harmonize better.

- **Material:** Use a light-colored shade to illuminate a space—say in a dark corner of a reading room—or to balance a dark lamp base. Likewise, lighter shades look good against the contrast of a dark wall. Use a darker shade for ambient lighting and dramatic effect in a light room. Choose texture and pattern in the same way you would for accent pillows and accessories—to enhance, but not detract.

- **Cleaning:** As with any other decorative accent pieces in the home, lamp shades benefit from a periodic cleaning. Fabric shades can be gently vacuumed using a brush attachment. "Fuzzy dusters" work well to get into the nooks and valleys of pleated-form plastic shades. Shades made of harder materials

or glass benefit from an occasional wipe with a dampened soft cloth.

How To...
Update a Countertop

Laminate countertops were once the material of choice for use in kitchens. These countertops—which have a wooden base to which a plastic-type sheet has been bonded—offered amazing choices for homeowners interested in adding color and pattern to a room.

However, those colors that were once "up-to-the-minute" in terms of style—avocado green, anyone?—can appear sadly out of date years later.

Options for countertop surfaces abound today. Choices include everything from newer laminates in up-to-date colors and designs to solid-surface countertops made of all one material, such as acrylic resins. Additional options include ceramic tile; stones, including marble, granite, and soapstone; butcher block woods; stainless steel, and even concrete! Prices for these countertops vary

widely from relatively inexpensive to high-cost, but also high impact.

Replacing a dated countertop is the best option for giving a kitchen an updated look without structural remodeling. However, if replacing your laminate countertops doesn't fit either your budget or your time at the moment, there are temporary solutions that will give you a better look for a time.

For instance, professional faux painter Kathryn Vork Waryan updated her aging 1950s laminate countertops with a faux paint treatment. Remember, since this is a painted surface, it is more subject to scratches and other damage than the original laminate was. In addition, painted countertops must be treated far more carefully than a more durable, newer alternative. Hot pans can never be set on this surface, nor can you cut on it. Food preparation must always be done on a separate surface, such as a cutting board.

That said, if you'd like to try this technique, first you'll need to clean the countertop extremely well. The sur-

face must be immaculate, with no dirt, grease, or other foreign material present. After scrubbing the counter, follow by washing the entire surface with a soft cloth and mineral spirits to ensure that no residue remains.

The most important step in this project is to prep the countertop with an excellent quality primer, designed to bond to laminates. A product called B-I-N, made by the Zinsser Company, (www.zinsser.com) is a shellac-based primer designed to adhere to laminates and other materials without prior sanding. Follow all manufacturer's instructions when using this product and let the primer dry thoroughly.

In Vork Waryan's kitchen, after priming the surfaces, she applied a base coat of latex paint and let it dry for four hours. Next she applied a faux treatment with latex paint by brushing the paint onto cut-up plastic bags and then laying them on the surface, pulling them up repeatedly for an attractive and easy faux finish. She finished the treatment with a freehand painting of fruit and flowers.

Once you've painted your counters, it's extremely important to seal the dried faux finish with several coats of a hard, durable, clear sealer.

Vork Waryan sealed her counter surface with several coats of Benjamin Moore's Stays Clear Acrylic Polyurethane Low Lustre, following the manufacturer's directions.

How To...
Prevent Sun Damage

Sunlight brightens any home, but those beautiful rays can fade carpeting, furniture, and window treatments. These tips will help you minimize the burn.

Who doesn't love a sun-filled home, with shining natural wood and colors that show up in all their splendor? After all, a bright day brings out the best in rooms filled with your favorite things. Or does it?

Sunshine sure perks up the mood of a room, but it can also change your attitude when you discover those sunbeams are ruining your furnishings.

Windows in a home do filter out enough of the sun's damaging rays to protect people's skin, but plain glass still admits 40 percent of the sun's ultraviolet (UV) rays. The light and heat of those rays can cause wood furnishings and floors to crack and fade, and they can also bleach and discolor fabrics, upholstery, rugs, artwork, and other possessions.

Many good solutions exist to help you prevent interior sun damage, however, and most of these techniques are also easy and economical. The easiest solution is also the cheapest—keep furniture and artwork out of direct sunlight and rotate area rugs whenever possible. Limit the amount of time an object is exposed to direct sun and you will obviously also minimize the amount of damage those sunbeams will do.

However, when that option proves impractical, there are other steps you can take to lessen the "sunburn" in your home.

You can control the amount of sunlight entering your home by focusing on exterior solutions, such as landscaping, or interior solutions, such as special window treatments or adding protective film directly to window glass. In addition, many quality fabrics and rugs already provide some fade-resistance through chemicals added during their manufacture.

Really, any preventative measure you take will be far better than the options you're left with once your belongings are damaged. Sun damage can be prevented, but it can't be reversed or quickly remedied with a miracle solution.

From the Outside In

Shading the outside of your home is an important and effective first defense against interior sun damage. If the sun can't stream directly in your windows, it can't fade your belongings.

Strategic landscaping, along with the use of awnings, patio covers, solar screens, and specialty windows all can help control the amount of light entering your home. The added benefit of these exterior solutions is energy efficiency and reduced heating and cooling expenses.

A few simple landscaping guidelines will help shade windows, but these are obviously longer-term solutions. To shade windows, plant deciduous trees with high, spreading branches and leaves on the south side of your home. Shrubs planted a few feet from all sides of the house also offer sun protection. A slightly quicker option for especially difficult areas such as south-facing windows is to place quick-growing vines and climbing plants in containers at those areas, letting the plants soak up the sun that might otherwise damage your interiors.

Awnings and patio covers also provide an excellent defense against harsh sunlight and can reduce heat gain in your home by nearly 80 percent. Like landscaping, these products are dual-purpose in that they provide shade for both the interior and exterior of the home, making both environments more comfortable and efficient. A benefit, though, that these products have over landscaping is that many awnings and patio covers are conveniently adjustable or retractable, so you can customize them to suit your particular climate and seasons.

Another option is to install solar screens on either the exterior or interior of your windows. These screens look much like standard window screens, but they can block up to 85 percent of the sun's rays from entering your home. The screens also reduce heat and glare, and they give you the option of opening your windows for fresh air without compromising sun protection. In addition, most solar screens can be customized, letting you make choices about the interior or exterior frame color. These screens also provide varying

Beautiful sunlight can fade your furnishings' color and luster. Prevent the damage!

Sunlight need not ruin any room.

degrees of opaqueness, for either increased visibility or privacy, and they can be built to fit any window opening, including arches and circles.

Updating your windows is yet another option when it comes to preventing damaging sunlight. New glass technologies provide increasingly sophisticated options for energy efficiency. For example, a typical, old, clear single-pane glass window blocks less than 25 percent of ultraviolet light and less than 15 percent of solar heat from entering your home. Fortunately, more advanced glass options are now on the market, which dramatically improve on these ratios.

According to the Efficient Windows Collaborative, sponsored by the U.S. Department of Energy, the advanced glazing systems available now include double- and triple-pane windows with coatings such as low-emissivity (low-e), spectrally selective, heat-absorbing (tinted), or reflective; gas-filled windows; and windows incorporating combinations of these options. Coatings on glass can reduce by three-quarters the amount of ultraviolet light entering your home. For further protection, ultraviolet absorbers can be incorporated to raise the protection from ultraviolet light to 99 percent or better.

To find out more about these special technologies, see sources below.

Fighting Fading on the Inside

Although the above-mentioned techniques will help minimize sun damage, you also need an interior strategy to protect furnishings and flooring. Consider options for window treatments including drapery, blinds, shades, sheers, or window film.

"Choosing an interior window treatment is more about aesthetics than sun protection, at this point," says Barbara Schlattman, FASID, an interior designer in Houston, Texas.

"There are so many different options available, but I prefer the window film. It can be transparent or tinted, reduces glare, protects the furnishings, and still allows the beauty of the outdoors to be part of your indoor environment."

Basically, as long as a window treatment blocks or sufficiently filters incoming sunlight, the right choice is in the eye of the beholder.

Solar Window film is an excellent option for controlling interior sunlight, glare, and heat. Film can be combined with any of the other exterior or interior protective solutions, resulting in almost complete protection from damaging ultraviolet rays and greatly increased energy efficiency. Many different types of window films are readily available. Purchasing the film in most cases will be quite easy, but proper installation is probably best left to a professional.

Once you're equipped with a little knowledge about how to control sunlight and heat, along with access to a marketplace full of innovative products and professionals, you can confidently sit back and enjoy your sunlit rooms—the gleaming wood, sparkling glass, vibrant colors, and playful reflections.

FOR MORE INFORMATION:

Efficient Windows Collaborative
www.efficientwindows.org

International Window Film Association
www.iwfa.com

Phifer Sun Control Products (solar screens)
www.phifer.com

U.S. Department of Energy
www.energy.gov

California Energy Commission
www.energy.ca.gov

Solar Screens Plus
www.solarscreensplus.com

How To...
Clean and Repair Grout

Have you been turning a blind eye to those dingy spaces between your floor, counter, or tub tiles?

"Chances are you haven't noticed your grout, unless it needs cleaning or repair," says Eric Astrachan, technical service manager at the Tile Council of America. "Grout either blends in with or frames out tiles, while holding them together and sealing out moisture and soil. When grout becomes stained or cracked, it turns tiled surfaces into an eyesore."

To fix grout in ceramic tile surfaces, the Tile Council of America recommends the following:

• **Cleaning:** Clean up spills as soon as possible. Regularly remove soil with a broom or vacuum. Sponge clean with water and a non-soap solution, which will prevent soap buildup and mildew problems. Thoroughly rinse all areas with clean warm water, and use a wet-or-dry vacuum, if possible. For stubborn stains, scrub the grout with a professional cleaning product. Follow specific product instructions.

• **Replacing:** When grout is cracked or stained beyond repair, you may need to replace it. Always start repairs in an unobtrusive place, and work in one small area at a time. Scrape out old grout with a grout saw and sponge.

Refill the area with new grout, following the product instructions.

• **Protecting:** Select a quality penetrating sealer, and apply as directed.

Note that procedures may be different for treating the grout in natural stone tiles, such as marble. Check with the product manufacturer before treating any stone surfaces.

1 Use a grout saw to remove damaged grout.

2 Force grout into joints with a rubber grout float held at a 45-degree angle.

3 Remove excess grout with a damp sponge. Allow to dry 30 minutes and wipe off any haze with a soft cloth.

4 Apply sealer with a clean sponge, sponge mop, or paint applicator. Allow to penetrate for 10 to 15 minutes.

5 Wipe off any sealer that hasn't been absorbed. Additional applications may be required. Let dry for 30 minutes between applications. When sealer no longer penetrates, the surface is sealed.

Index